TO TIMBUKTU

TO TIMBUKTU

A JOURNEY DOWN THE NIGER

MARK JENKINS

MODERN TIMES

Modern Times is a trademark of Rodale Inc.

Rodale books may be purchased for business or promotional
use or for special sales. For information, please write to:

Special Markets Department, Rodale, Inc., 733 Third Avenue,
New York, NY 10017

Printed in the United States of America

Rodale Inc. makes every effort to use acid-free a, recycled paper o .

Map on page x Quill/William Morrow

Previous editions of *To Timbuktu* published by:

A. W. Bruna Uitgevers (Holland), 1997, paperback, ISBN 90–229–8357–9
Frederking & Thaler (Germany), 1997, paperback, ISBN 3–89405–144–0
William Morrow, 1997, hardcover, ISBN 0–688–11585–3
Biblioteca Grandes Viajeros (Spain), 1998, paperback, ISBN 84–406–8385–5
Quill/William Morrow, 1998, paperback, ISBN 0–688–16342–4
Robert Hale (England), 1998, hardcover, ISBN 0–7090–6151–X
Sirene Pockets (Holland), 2000, paperback, ISBN 90–5831–057–4
Robert Hale (England), 2002, paperback, ISBN 0–7090–7296–1
National Geographic Adventure Press/Frederking & Thaler (Germany),
    2007, paperback, ISBN 978–3–894–5–114–3

Library of Congress Cataloging-in-Publication Data

Jenkins, Mark, date
    To Timbuktu : a journey down the Niger / Mark Jenkins.
        p.   cm.
    ISBN-13 978–1–59486–765–1 paperback
    ISBN-10 1–59486–765–8 paperback
    1. Niger River—Description and travel.   2. Jenkins, Mark, date—
Travel—Guinea.   3. Jenkins, Mark, date—Travel—Mali.   4. Kayak
touring—Niger River.   5. Kayak touring—Guinea.   6. Kayak touring—
Mali.   7. Tombouctou (Mali)—Description and travel.   I. Title.
DT360.J46 2008
916.6204'3—dc22   2008009829

Distributed to the trade by Macmillan

2   4   6   8   10   9   7   5   3   1   paperback

FOR MOM AND DAD
AND MIKE MOE

A BOY'S WILL IS THE WIND'S WILL,
AND THE THOUGHTS OF YOUTH ARE LONG, LONG THOUGHTS

—HENRY WADSWORTH LONGFELLOW

CONTENTS

ix

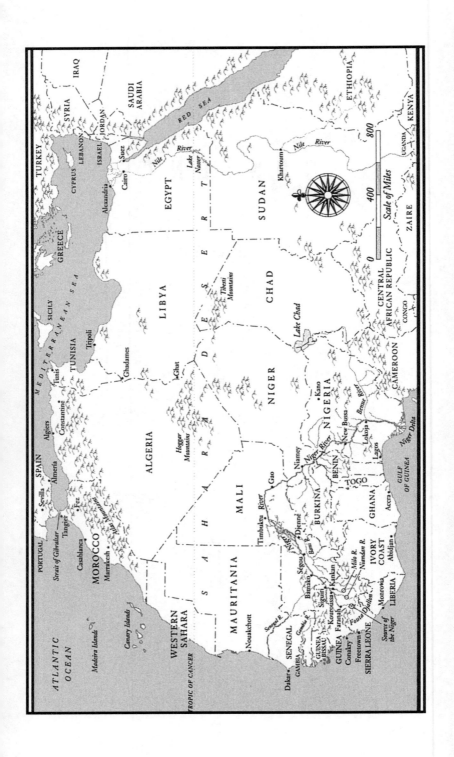

TO TIMBUKTU

EDDIES

I am moving but can't see where I'm going. The river is bearing me. The prow of my boat cleaves folds of whiteness and pulls me through. My course is invisible but I keep paddling, steadily dipping the blades side to side. The cadence keeps me balanced.

The fog came in the night, dampening the thirsty earth, stilling the howling cicadas. We were too tired to notice it. Dead atop our sleeping bags, insects gnawing at the netting, sweating in our sleep, dreaming murky, disjointed parables as all white people dream here. In the morning we crawled out of our tents and the river was gone. We squatted silently in the mud like the Africans and ate the last of our food. Then we broke camp, loaded our boats, and pressed them like scalpels into the flesh of the river.

At first we tried to paddle in formation—single file down the middle of the river, gunboats staggered. Me in front as point man, on the lookout for crocs and hippos, sidearm on my lap; Rick next, then Mike with his gun, John taking up the rear. But the mist was too thick. One by one we were swallowed.

No matter. We are all going down the same river together even if we are lost to each other.

There are no rapids in this section, only arcing ribs of current disappearing into the ghostly void. It is deceptive. The surface of a river is only the skin, the muscle is underneath. You can't know this from shore. You must be out in a small boat; then you know it because you feel it. We are in kayaks, the smallest of vessels. In a kayak you are not above the river, you are inside it, part of it. Water envelops you and carries you on your voyage.

We are running higher in the water than normal because we have eaten our ballast. We left the last village loaded to the gunwales. The women came down to the river with their baskets balanced on their heads. They were colorful and gay as tall flowers. Worms of mud pressed up between their toes. We bought oranges and bananas and cassava and tins of Moroccan sardines and distributed the weight between fore and aft hatches. The French bread was a surprise. We took the whole basket, strapping the tan limbs to our decks as if we were cannibals.

Now it is all gone and our boats are lithe and nimble again. I feel free, like a plane in the clouds. But I know better. Water is not like air. Although I am the helmsman and may pilot left or right or even swirl myself in circles, my true direction is chosen by the river. My path is the path of the river.

The fog is starting to pull apart now. Bombs of sunlight are exploding on the surface of the water. I begin to pass through brilliant holes of light. Colors flash around me as if I were inside a kaleidoscope. I am so absorbed I don't realize Mike has appeared beside me. We must have been parallel. He doesn't speak. He glides in to starboard; we match strokes and ride like light cavalry through the discharges.

Around a wide bend Mike suddenly stops paddling and points with his blade. I look where he is looking. There is something ahead of us on the river, something moving through the shrouds. We take chase, our boats bounding through the water like dogs. We have no idea what we are after. Then we break into a clearing.

It is a man. He is poling a dugout across the river. The dugout is so deep in the river the man looks as if he is walking on water.

As we come closer, we can see him better. The sun is glancing off his shoulders. He is wearing rough shorts that hang from narrow hips. His body is knotted with muscle. He is standing with one leg forward and both hands on the pole, like a gondolier.

He is making his way from left to right across the river, drifting downstream. His movements are measured and efficient. He is nearing the shore and we are behind him, closing in, when he vanishes into the reeds. We wave our paddles and shout but he doesn't look back.

We enter the reeds at the place where we last saw him and follow a canal through thatched archways. At the end we find his dugout and wet footprints ascending steps cut in a mud bank. We climb out of our boats. On top of the bank there is a passageway through the elephant grass. It bends back and forth, penetrating deep into the bush, before emptying into a small opening.

In the enclosure are five men squatting on their haunches. The figure in the middle, an old man with kinky gray hair, is drawing with a stick in the dirt. The other men are watching him.

As we step from the tunnel, the men stand up and face us. The old man holds the stick at his side.

"*Bonjour,*" says Mike. His voice is cheerful but soft. He does not want to disturb whatever is happening.

They don't speak.

"*Eneeche,*" I say in Malinke, the tongue of this region.

Again they don't reply.

The men are all barechested, wearing only tattered shorts. They are dusty. Their stomachs are corrugated. They have deep chests. The veins in their long arms bulge and at the ends of their arms hang heavy, knuckled hands. Their legs are animal legs, lean and scarred. Their feet rough and caked with dirt.

Using words in French and Malinke Mike asks the men if there is a village nearby. He tells them we are out of food and hungry.

The men stand dead still and say nothing.

We point in different directions and watch for their reaction. Their heads do not turn.

3

Only one man has wet feet. He must be our boatman, our kin. I step toward him.

"*Nourriture?*" I point to my mouth and make the movements of eating. He does not respond and I look into his face.

Suddenly my eyes are jumping from face to face.

"Mike!"

"I know. I just figured it out."

The pupils of each man are solid white.

Mike is almost whispering. "They have river blindness."

"How did they get here?"

"He poled them across."

"How could he?"

"You saw him."

None of the men have moved. They are like wooden posts driven into the dirt, telamones supporting the weight of the African sky.

Mike kneels down and examines the picture the old man made in the ground with the stick.

"Mark, what is it?"

I stare at the drawing. There is a circle; inside the circle are several wavy horizontal lines. They remind me of running water.

"I don't know. Looks like a circle of water."

Mike stands up and we step back. There is nothing we can do. We leave. Back to the river.

Strange things happen in Africa. Fantastic things. Things you can't understand. You sense they portend something but you don't know what. Africans are accustomed to it. For them strangeness is commonplace. They don't try to decipher it. If they have a problem, they talk to a lawyer or an accountant or a shaman or a necromancer. Depends on the problem.

Back at our boats moored in the reeds, there is not enough room to turn around. We must back out. As we exit the channel, the river catches us amidships. Mike wheels his prow upstream and allows the force of the current to push him around. I don't spin myself about. I let my boat slide backward down the river.

We glide downstream together, Mike facing forward, me facing backward. Kayaks, being pointed at both ends, can travel in either direction with grace. We say little. We have been on many expeditions together. It is what we have done best together. We know there is plenty of time to talk—soon as you really have something to say. Mike and I usually talk at night, after the day has settled in, lying on our backs in the dark in the tent.

We stay close and let the river carry us where it will. Past the reeds, down around the next bend and out into open brown water. Then the current begins to slide us off toward the bank.

"I think we should wait for Rick and John."

Mike nods and flicks his wrist, splashing me with his paddle.

Instead of pulling ourselves back into the middle of the stream, we let the current continue to angle us toward shore. We are heading for an eddy.

I hit the eddyline first, riding astern up onto the ridge of turbulence. My boat begins jerking, the bow and stern snapping back and forth. I stroke hard to port until I've pulled myself over the edge into the smooth water. Immediately my boat is becalmed. For a moment I am motionless, held in suspension like a boy on a swing at the top of his arc. Then, almost imperceptibly, I begin to glide forward, upriver. I am inside the eddy.

Most people believe rivers flow in only one direction. This is not true. Along the margins of a river the water curls back on itself and runs upstream, as if it has forgotten something. The movement is particularly pronounced along the inside bank of sharp bends and directly behind boulders that split the current like a wedge. It's a natural phenomenon. Rivers only appear to be linear. Inside, rivers are recursive.

Mike follows me up onto the eddyline but instead of crossing over, he stops midway and begins to play. He doesn't fight the opposing currents, he uses them, churning himself in circles.

The eddyline is where the two slabs of water, rushing in opposite directions, pass each other. It is a boundary. All the water inside this border, in the eddy, is bewitched and flows magically upstream. All the water beyond the eddyline flows downstream, like a river is supposed to.

Downstream is the direction most people go. That's what we are usually doing. Mike and I and Rick and John, four white guys from Wyoming paddling through black Africa. But there are people who go upstream. Some of them have kayaked the entire length of a river backward. They do it using the eddies, maneuvering upriver from one pool to the next, bucking the current in between, portaging around the waterfalls carrying their shells on their backs like turtles. Some have gone all the way to a river's source this way. It is arduous, but they have their reasons.

When you are descending a river, eddies are places where you can pull in and park. All rivers have them. To know where the eddies are is to know how to find tranquil water amid the ceaselessness. Eddies are a good place to rest, to look back upstream. Sometimes you can see farther ahead looking backward.

Mike is still dancing on the eddyline, his paddle held out like an acrobat's pole. He's practicing low braces, high braces, pirouettes, working the water. He's not interested in the reflective pool inside the eddy. If he didn't have so much gear strapped to the deck of his boat, I know he'd try a few rolls.

"Buck"—he's grinning at me—"did you ever think we'd end up here again?"

I am still facing backward, slipping upstream.

"Yes. You?"

"Yup."

We were working on the Eskimo roll before class. It was winter. The creeks and lakes around town were trapped under two feet of ice, so we were practicing in the pool.

The Eskimo roll is a fundamental maneuver in kayaking. Unlike all other boats man has invented, kayaks were designed to be rolled.

To hunt sea mammals through pack ice, maneuvering easily and swiftly along remote leads, Eskimos needed a craft as sleek and agile as their prey, something that could spin on a dime when a seal surfaced behind them. Consequently, they created a boat that was shaped like a seal—pointed at prow and stern, with a round, keelless belly. It was even sewn from sealskin. But a keelless boat is tipsy, so they cinched the deck tight around the paddler's waist. Now when the boat did tip over, it wouldn't swamp. The only trick was getting back up. It had to be done immediately. Humans freeze to death in a matter of minutes in Arctic water. Hence: the Eskimo roll. A smooth sweep of the paddle underwater, a quick flick of hip and knee, and presto, back to the surface like a cork.

Mike got it right away. Rolling in full circles slick as a seal. Water was his natural habitat. He was a state champion swimmer, a "fish" in high school patois. Round head, orange hair tinted lime from the chlorine, foot-deep chest. He moved through the sapphire liquid like a submarine. His lungs were so powerful he could swim three lengths of the pool underwater without coming up for air.

It wasn't so easy for me. I swam with the swim team to stay in shape, but I wasn't a "fish." I was a gymnast. At least that's the sport I competed in. What I loved was climbing mountains. Rock was my natural habitat. In the water I tended to muscle things and you can't muscle the Eskimo roll; it takes technique.

Mike made it look easy. He'd pretend he was shot and slowly fall over sideways, sink under, hang upside down from his boat for a second, then explode back up. He could even do it without a paddle, perfectly timing the thrust of his shoulders, sweep of his arms, and snap of his knee. It's called a combat roll.

An ordinary roll was enough for me. I usually hit it, but sometimes I had to bail—peeling out of the cockpit underwater, then ignominiously dogpaddling my capsized kayak to the side of the pool.

Of course we didn't make it easy on each other. That would have been unsporting. When one of us went under, the other would hold his boat down so he couldn't immediately roll back up. It got to be a game. Who could stay under longer.

After a while it became unnecessary to hold each other under; we did it to ourselves. Flipped over and just hung there, upside down underwater. This is an unnatural position for humans. You get disoriented beneath the water with your head pointing down. You can't breathe so you start to panic. Your lungs begin to burn and your heart starts thundering and your brain misfires and suddenly a chemical fear is coursing through your body. Adrenaline, pure animal instinct. Fight or flight—roll or bail. We were trying to teach ourselves how not to do both. How to control fear. After a while we weren't practicing the Eskimo roll anymore; we were practicing sangfroid.

One morning Coach caught us.

Coach was a compassionate, taciturn, merciless man. He looked like Clint Eastwood. He led the swim team to seven consecutive state titles. He was one of the few people on earth who expected more from himself than from you. Kids swam hard for Coach, swam to guthollow, limplimbed, red-eyed exhaustion.

With Coach there were different punishments for different crimes. If you pushed a kid into the pool, a minor offense, you'd get a few thousand yards. Snap someone with a towel leaving a welt big enough for Coach to notice, and after confessing, you'd get laps plus weights. For serious transgressions—arrogance, vanity, pride, or hubris—your sentence was something special. The Hallelujah.

There was a ritual to the Hallelujah. The guilty had to wait for an unforewarned day. It was always conducted directly following workout when you were already beat. No kids who couldn't take it ever got it.

We got it a week later. Coach blew the whistle and we all

climbed out to shower and crawl into our clothes and bicycle home and fall asleep in our dinner plates, then he turned to us.

"Jenkins. Moe. Back in the pool."

We knew what to do. We dove back in and began treading water in the deep end under the diving board. Coach slowly walked down the length of the pool and stepped up onto the board. He moved out to the end, seated himself with his legs crossed like a black belt, which he was, and peered down at us.

Already the pool was strangely calm after suffering three hours of flogging. As if it were flesh preternaturally closing over a wound.

"You two like to push it, don't you."

We grinned up at him like the adolescent fools we were.

"Okay. I want you to imagine that your hands are tied to a pole above your head."

We understood. We'd been here before. Even if it was the first time for some poor sucker, he would have already heard the rumors and would know what to do. We raised our arms up into the air.

"Elbows out of the water, gentlemen."

To tread water using both your arms and legs is not hard. You rotate your arms in wide flat ovals and frog-kick your legs one at a time. Everything is synchronized and your head stays well above the surface of the water. With practice you can do it for a long time.

To tread water without your arms, with your arms not only useless but raised above your head as extra weight, is different. You must frog-kick strenuously, but if you kick too hard, as if you're frightened that you might drown, you become exhausted within minutes and your head starts to go under and you do begin to drown. So there's a method. First you must lean your head back until your eyes are staring straight up at the ceiling. At the same time you must allow yourself to sink until only your face is above the surface. Then you must kick only enough to keep your mouth from filling with water. The liquid will be all around your face, splashing into the corners of your eyes, but you must stay calm.

We frog-kicked with our arms up in the air and Coach sat there. He did not say things to make us angry or inspire us. He simply sat there, above us.

For the first few minutes Mike and I razzed Coach. We shouted at him about how easy it was, how we could do it all night, how he should go out and get us a pizza so we could eat it while we were treading water.

Coach smiled.

We clapped our hands and shouted. We clapped our hands in unison as if we were at a rock concert. We sang lewd songs.

This didn't last long. Shenanigans used up too much strength. Besides, something else starts to happen after your body has been moving in a slow, powerful rhythm for a while: Your mind is set free. Your body is operating on its own, autonomous and self-governing, so you can go anywhere you want.

I don't know where Mike went, but I went off to Europe.

When I was thirteen, my family had moved to Holland. Just picked up and left. Mom and Dad were from the limitless ocean of South Dakota and had wanted to sail away since they met. Then I came along. Then Steve. Then Pam and Dan and Wendy Sue and Christopher. By then they had it figured out. Go even if you can't possibly go. Even if it will take a miracle.

We only lived in de Nederland for one year but nothing was ever the same again. We were just dirt and snow kids from the high plains of Wyoming when the rest of the world got lodged inside us like an arrowhead too close to the spine. I started dreaming about Europe the day we got back. I dreamed about it at night and daydreamed about it in class. This had been going on for three years. I got so good at slipping off to Europe I could get there in a matter of seconds.

So I was somewhere on a nude beach with a medieval castle doing heroic things when a wave of fatigue spilled over me and I realized that soon I wouldn't be able to talk anymore.

"Mike?"

"Buck?"

"I been thinking about escaping."

"Yeah."

"You want to go?"

"Sure. Where're we going?"

"Europe."

We had to stop talking after that. We had to conserve our energy.

We treaded through seconds and minutes. We treaded through dinnertime, our stomachs sucking up into our ribs. We treaded through pieces of memory that slipped away before we could find out what they were.

After a while everything started to turn blue. A deep melting blue. The water. The air. The concrete ceiling. The underside of the diving board. Even our arms drooping above our heads like limbs in a Salvador Dali painting.

Then we went past the point when you think you are too tired to go on for another second so you close your eyes and try to make time disappear. But even then, even when it started getting rough, it wasn't that bad really because Coach was right there. Right above our heads. He still is.

And time did disappear. It had to.

Just when we were empty, our arms still hanging on to the air but our legs sinking as if tied to cement blocks and our heads quietly going under, Coach spoke. We could hardly hear him.

"Hit the showers."

The day school got out we went down to the railroad office. We stood in line in workboots and workclothes and lowered baseball caps and lied through our teeth. We lied about our ages and our experience and fabricated Social Security numbers and the man spit lassos of tobacco juice on our feet and didn't believe a word but didn't give a damn either because he was shorthanded up in Medicine Bow.

It was a rail gang. We worked thirteen twelves—twelve hours a day, thirteen days on, one day off. Using crowbars and hand jacks we raised and straightened track buckled and splayed by the coal trains heaving down from Hanna. We were the only white guys on the crew. They called us *güeros* and *pendejos* and *cabrones* but we didn't give a shit because they were lifers and we were going to escape. They were working on the railroad out in the freezing burning prairie. We were working on the underground railroad, digging a tunnel out of Wyoming.

After we'd each saved a thousand bucks, enough to go clear around the world, we quit. Just packed up our tent and walked away with a roll of twenties bulging in our pockets like hard-ons.

Mike was a year ahead and had graduated that spring. I finished high school by Christmas, a semester early. For graduation Mom and Dad and the kids gave me a one-way bus ticket to New York City and Mike bought his own and our families came to the bus station to see us off. They waved at us and we waved at them until we lost each other in the whirling snow.

It was January 1977. Mike and I were eighteen.

Of course we didn't know it then, but there are only certain times in your life when you can do certain things. If you don't do them that very moment, they pass you by forever and you and your life become something else. Lighting out to see the world is one of those things. If you are too young, you will be hurt by the malformed people who prey on innocents, and never again feel safe or trust humans. If you are too old, the seeds of cynicism and fearfulness have already taken root and you shall be a loathsome traveler. You must be young enough to believe in your own immortality in a mysterious, ineluctable way, but old enough to understand that you could die if you got too messed up.

Sitting in the front seats of the bus staring at the storm burying the highway and the sagebrush and the antelope,

Mike and I were trembling from an untaintable, undauntable expectancy.

It was still snowing when we landed in Europe. We couldn't believe the prices. We'd already shot half our wad on the plane ticket. We decided not to spend another dime of our hard-earned dinero. We'd live off the land. We set out on foot and walked across Luxembourg in one day, once taking refuge in a pub where old men in berets bought us mugs of warm beer.

We hitchhiked to Paris expecting it to be as beautiful as a songbird, but instead it was winter there too. In spring, when you're supposed to go to Paris, it's probably beautiful and romantic but in winter it is sleeting and the city is as ugly as a wet pigeon. An old man with a teal cravat and a red nose bought us dinner one night because he remembered weeping when the Americans marched down the Champs Élysées. We drank port and he cried, "*Le plus beau jour pour la France!*" and it made him weep again. The police arrested us for camping in the Bois de Boulogne. Then again for camping in the Montparnasse cemetery.

In Barcelona we got mixed up in a riot and had to run from soldiers with shields beating people with truncheons and firing rubber bullets.

In Madrid we tried to hop a freight train but failed and wound up sleeping in flower beds. We found out it was easier to hop passenger trains and just hide from the conductor. Once we fell in with some sailors and got so drunk we got off at different stations and didn't find each other for a couple of days.

In the south of Spain we fell in love and then left before dawn because we were going and they were staying and we thought that was the biggest difference there was.

We were having fun but Europe wasn't the adventure I'd remembered as a boy. I'd thought I knew where we were going but when we got there it was gone. Europe wasn't a mysterious land full of opportunities for valor and hardship. Europe was more like America's grandfather. Old and familiar with a few quirky traditions. That's not what we wanted. We didn't leave Wyoming to wind up at Grandpa's. We left home to be homeless. To be fugitives.

One afternoon while we were walking along the docks sharing half a loaf of bread we'd found on a bench and staring out at the ruffling green sea, it hit us.

Africa.

It was a word from the boundlessness of childhood. Big and deep as the sky. We couldn't believe we hadn't thought of it earlier.

That same evening we boarded a rusty cargo transport and slammed out into the Mediterranean. It was a bad ship and we got caught in a bad storm. Seawater gushed across the floor and the hull thundered and bowed and we thought we were going down. Greengilled, gritting our teeth, we clung all night long to our slatmetal beds.

But at dawn we stepped off the gangplank as if onto a new planet.

Tattooed women gorgeous as knives. Children innocent as ducklings flopping in the street with mangled wings. Upside down sheep screaming then coughing then quiet. Muezzins wailing, blind men moaning. Radios cutting tin with a dull saw. Pyramids of oranges and dates and olives. Goat heads and sheep heads and shark heads. Entrails of everything. Catacombs of homes. Camels. Hooded men in djellabas drinking mint tea in the shadows. Thieves with daggers tailing us like jackals.

We were exultant, insane with triumph. We'd made our getaway. Given our home on the range the slip and flung ourselves halfway around the world.

To celebrate we decided to splurge and buy a map of Africa. The map was too expensive so I distracted the clerk for Mike. Clean as a whistle. We walked straight out of town, nicking a few oranges along the way. An hour later we dropped off the road and hid behind a grove of trees. After we were certain we weren't being followed, Mike got out the map.

When he unfolded it, an entire continent blossomed before our eyes. We stared at the vastness of this unknown land for several minutes before speaking.

14

"Hey, look at this."

Mike leaned over my finger and read a tiny word almost lost in the blankness.

"Tom-bouct-ou?"

"Timbuktu!"

"I thought it was a myth."

"It's right there, man. Right on the other side of the desert."

We were two rubes from Wyoming on the lam in Africa. All we wanted was adventure. I got out a pencil and Mike drew a line straight south from Tangier to Timbuktu.

Heraclitus said you can never step into the same river twice. He traveled in Africa around 500 BC and decided life was all motion and flux so it was impossible. And maybe it is. But people do it all the time. We are magical beings. We become what we are.

Late one night, fourteen years later, I called Mike. I was afraid to wake Diana but he picked up the phone before it even rang, as if we were identical twins.

"Michael, I'm looking at the atlas."

"Well, whaddaya know," he rattled a stiff page into the receiver.

"Things are going to change soon."

"Yup. Forever."

We were about to become fathers. My wife, Sue, and his wife, Diana, were both pregnant, their due dates only two weeks apart.

I asked him what continent he was looking at.

"Asia. What about you?"

"Africa."

"Hmm."

"So what'll it be? Mountain or river?"

"I'm thinking river this time."

Mike's last trip had been a sea kayaking journey off the Wild Coast of the Transkei in South Africa. My last had

15

been a mountain climbing expedition in Bolivia. Nothing had changed. Water was still Mike's element; mountains were mine.

"I think I'm not much of a boatman, Mike."

"All the better. You know that. Ignorance—"

"—is the root of adventure."

We both cracked up.

Once upon a time we were in a bar in Alaska slaphappy with ourselves for having lived through another misadventure. We were badly sunburned and partially frostbitten and hadn't bathed for several weeks. The bartender was a gorgeous Czech with big tits and a green V-necked sweater to show them off. We were doing all we could to impress her when she turned down her pouty red lips and said in her exquisite Slavic accent, "You know boyz, *ignoraince* iz ze rroot of adventure." It was supposed to be a put-down but we were just drunk enough to be honest with ourselves. We decided she was right and made a toast as she sashayed away.

"We don't have much time."

"Enough."

We didn't say any more. Didn't have to. What we had to do was talk to our wives.

In the morning I had toast buttered and cut corner-to-corner and was pouring a glass of juice when Sue appeared in her nightgown. She sat down at the kitchen table rubbing her eyes, looked at the toast, then at me.

"Okay. What's up?"

"How'd you sleep?"

She smiled and touched my arm. "Mark, where are you going?"

I had made one or two or three trips a year since we'd met. Unlike all other women I'd known, Sue understood they were not something I would grow out of.

"I called Mike last night."

"I knew you got up again."

I had started slipping out of bed after I thought Sue had fallen asleep, dressing in the hallway, stepping outside and going for long walks in the dark.

Sometimes Sue and I traveled together, but when I left and she stayed, she didn't pine away. She went on about her life. She did all the things she wanted to do. Once, after I'd spent a half year bicycling across Russia, she'd moved to another town in another state. I returned home to a home I'd never seen, a woman I hardly knew. She had new friends and a new life. I was the one who left. Leaving is easy. Coming home and trying to fit back in is the hard part.

"What do you think? Will you be okay?"

"Of course, pregnancy's not an injury."

She was still running five miles a day and had just won a biathlon on a team called Two Girls and a Guy. Still, she was starting to take catnaps in the afternoon, trying to get me to lie down with her. Mike said Diana was sleeping on the couch because it was more comfortable.

"All you have to—"

"Never have and never will. Where are you going?"

"We don't know yet."

"What are you doing?"

"We're not sure."

She leaned across the kitchen table and kissed my neck. "Let's hope you have a clue before you leave."

Mike came over later that morning. He and Diana had talked. He told me that when they got married they had made a pact—he was allowed one trip every two years, no more.

"But somehow I didn't do one last year," he said, grinning ear to ear and snapping his fingers like a Gypsy.

If it was to be a river, then it should be a remote river, a river whose source was unknown or at least a good mystery. This would ensure a search—something we'd figured out long ago was more important and more fun than whatever one is searching for.

It should also be a river whose headwaters, the first few hundred miles of water, were unknown. The lower reaches of a river didn't matter. They are always fat and flat and domesticated, continually plowed by ferries and freighters. We wanted to navigate the unnavigable—that wild young race in the mountains—and, we wanted to be the first.

Now the desire to be the first at anything is regularly ridiculed. Usually it is dismissed as adolescent and gauche, a callow desire for fame. And sometimes it is. But as most people find out, the fantasy of fame, when you're in the jungle of struggle, is too feckless to carry you through.

What does being the first really mean? It means no road map. It means that you'll have to figure things out on your own. Some people enjoy this, some people don't. Once something has been explored, there's a path. The next person to get there takes the path. He doesn't have to create the path—someone else did that for him. The experience of trying to create the path is what those who desire to be first actually desire. Physicists, violinists, explorers. Pundits and pedants, traveling as they are on well-worn paths, can't help but miss the point.

Mike and I began making phone calls.

The Chinese embassy, polite and brittle as china, said there was no country called Tibet, but for a fee of "one million dollar" they would happily issue a stamped slip of wax paper giving us permission to boat a mile or two of the Brahmaputra. The Afghan embassy said running the Helmand might be ticklish because it was a main trade route for poppies, each bend of the river owned by a warlord armed with rocket launchers. The Burmese government said the northern half of their country was closed due to "internal things not to do with anybody else." When we pressed them about the Irrawaddy and the Salween, they said that if we did somehow get onto one of their rivers we would meet an "unfortunate problem."

We switched to Africa. The Nile and the Congo were already out. They'd been run. Same with the Orange River in South Africa. The Okavango and the Zambezi were options, but their upper reaches were in Angola. The Angolan embassy claimed their war was "essentially over, yes mostly over," although the particular region we were interested in was still experiencing "sporadic slaughter."

That left one major river: the Niger. We put in a few calls to river rats, guys who had boated all over the world. A Frenchman named Henri Lhoti had kayaked the middle sections in the 1940s, as had a German named Achiel Mozer in the mid-1980s. But: The headwaters were still unexplored.

We studied the atlas. The Niger is Africa's third largest river. Over three thousand miles long, it arcs across the chest of West Africa like the tattoo of a question mark—rising in the mountains of the Fouta Djallon in western Guinea, running north across Mali into the Sahara, then suddenly hooking south, passing through Niger, Benin, and Nigeria before emptying into the Gulf of Guinea.

I dialed the number of the Guinean embassy.

"Permits? For the Niger?" She had a British accent sweetened by the singsong lilt of an African tongue. "What in the world for? You will most certainly be killed."

"How?"

"Eaten alive I should guess."

I asked her what would be stupid enough to eat something as tasteless as a human. She was taken aback.

"My fine young man. If you had done even a farthing's worth of research you would know that the hippopotamus, a seemingly docile and shy creature, is actually a temperamental beast that kills more people than any other animal in Africa."

"Other than our own species," I said.

"Quite," she said.

"Thank you very much," I said.

"Not at all," she said.

We called the Malian embassy.

"Ah, but gentlemahn, gentlemahn," sang a diplomat, "I must say that in all my life I have never heard of such a foolhardy notion. But, if you truly wish to take your little boats and ride them down the mighty Niger, we don't mind at all. It is your skin, isn't it?"

That settled it. Mike was already zipping out checklists. We were both talking at once. There's nothing on earth like a good Huck Finn adventure to turn full-grown men right back into boys.

"Canoes?"

"Kayaks."

"They'll have to be big to carry all the gear."

"They'll have to be foldables to get them to the headwaters."

"What about malaria?"

"Chloroquine's not working anymore. Resistant strains. We'll have to get Lariam. How about machetes?"

"Let's get them there. Infection?"

"Tetracycline. Amoxicillin. Maybe some Keflex."

In the space of twelve hours it was happening again, the undertaking of a grand undertaking. It's like falling in love: Once you get that girl in your head, from then on no matter what you think you're thinking about you're thinking about her. You're obsessed. You just hear her name and your ears stretch to the size of paddles and the bats take off in your stomach.

We made hundreds of phone calls and checked out dozens of books and maps and stayed up till all hours and never thought twice because we were planning another adventure. It was natural. In the warmth of your own kitchen pluck and mettle flow as easily as tap water. You don't and won't have to account for your hubris until you're out there—when it's too late to turn back or take it back and all you can really do is muddle through and pray that when it comes to a pinch you still have the balls you thought you had.

After you've done a number of such trips, you know that you may actually be planning your own death. But you don't think of it that way. You can't; otherwise you'd never go. You think of it as an opportunity. A chance to ride the swift-flying arrow of your own desire. When doubt rises up like a cold fog around your heart, you pull out the maps again.

Maps encourage boldness. They're like cryptic love letters. They make anything seem possible. Maps impart an order to the earth, flattening a hurling space into safe, two-dimensional squares with borders and straight lines. Mountains with heights, oceans with depths. Of course when you get there, it's nothing like what you thought it would be. It's as if a bomb went off just before you arrived and everything is chaos and you have no idea what's going on.

Books are more accurate but leave less to the imagination. They are three-dimensional, full of flawed people like yourself. Of course the authors are flawed too. Biased in ways that they try to hide, idiosyncratic in ways they try to champion. You learn to read between the lines.

I always start with the journals of the explorers. They're useful but you have to distinguish between what's really happening and what you're being told is happening. Explorers have a difficult time with this. They're usually too close to the action to make a fair judgment. That's the task of historians—they have the benefit of the unknown and terrible future already having become the tamed undangerous past.

Herodotus died in 425 BC with his book unfinished. As a youth he had traveled and fought and lived wild, and in his old age he sat down to write about what he had seen and heard.

In his book Herodotus told a tale of young Berber warriors crossing an immense desert and finding a great river on the other side. The river was teeming with crocodiles and gigantic gray water horses. The warriors said the river flowed east. Herodotus believed this unknown river to be an eastern branch of the Nile.

In the first century AD, Pliny the Elder, in his thirty-seven-volume *Natural History*, concurred with Herodotus: The mysterious river south of the great desert ran east. Its name was the Niger, which came from the word *n'ger*, which in the language of the desert nomads meant, simply, "river."

In the next century Ptolemy wrote his book *Guide to Geography*. In it he drew a map of Africa. He disagreed with Herodotus and Pliny; he had the Niger running west and emptying into the Atlantic.

A thousand years later Al-Idrisi wrote *The Book of Roger*, named in honor of his benefactor, King Roger II of Sicily. Al-Idrisi sided with Ptolemy. The Niger flowed west.

In 1353, Ibn Battutu, the greatest traveler of the millennium, crossed the desert to reach the enigmatic Niger. Battutu paddled down the river in a dugout himself, so he was quite certain: the Niger flowed east.

As far as history was concerned, the Niger, a river named *river*, flowed in two directions. It was one half of the greatest geographical conundrum of the Western world. The other half was the persistent rumor of a golden city on the banks of the Niger.

In 1324 a magnificent caravan had appeared out of the desert in Egypt. It stretched for miles in the liquid heat, leather armor clattering, spears piercing the sky, flags popping. Its grandeur was unimaginable. Five hundred barefoot slaves wielding staffs of solid gold; towering camels so laden with gold they stumbled in the sand. Mansa Musa, emperor of Mali, had crossed the Sahara.

Mansa Musa was on a pilgrimage, a spiritual quest, like all true travelers. He was bound for Mecca. This did not interest the inhabitants of Egypt. *Gold* is what interested them. Musa told them he and his gold were from someplace far, far away. A city called Timbuktu.

Word of this gilded Atlantis lost in an ocean of sand slowly spread. From the ports of Egypt across the Mediterranean to the ports of Italy, France, and Spain, whence it flowed like alcohol into the veins of Europe, intoxicating the young and the brave.

Leo Africanus was one man who got drunk on the myth and set off for Africa. He spent several years there between

1510 and 1518, thus his historical sobriquet. When he returned home, he wrote his own book, *History and Description of Africa and the Notable Things Contained Therein*. He confirmed the unbelievable. He said the citizens of Timbuktu were enormously rich. He said the king of Timbuktu had scepters of gold weighing more than ten men. Furthermore, he said, he had boated down the Niger himself and it most definitely flowed west.

In 1590 the sultan of Morocco sent out an expedition of five thousand camel-mounted cavalry and two thousand foot soldiers. He couldn't have cared less about the recursive river; he wanted the gold. The expedition's mission: cross the Sahara, take Timbuktu. Which, after great losses, they did. And for a few years an occasional caravan straggled back to Morocco loaded with loot and tribute. But the city was too remote to hold. The soldiers interbred and the caravans stopped.

In 1618 the British, mariners perforce of their geography, sent two expeditions up an unknown river on the west coast of Africa. The sailors thought they might actually be on the Niger. Both vessels cruised between the impenetrable, rotting green banks expecting the promised land around every bend. Neither found it. One ship returned with fantastic tales of a city whose houses were roofed with gold. One ship, and all its crew, was never heard from again.

Two centuries passed with no new knowledge about the Niger or Timbuktu. A renowned English botanist who had been on Captain Cook's first voyage, Sir Joseph Banks, found this lack of progress intolerable. By God, this was the age of Enlightenment. He himself had collected plants in Brazil, Australia, Tahiti, and New Zealand. It was ridiculous that much of the world was already so well explored and yet no one had penetrated the Dark Continent just a few thousand miles south of England.

In 1788, Banks organized a gentlemen's club composed of a dozen of his cronies—lords, landlords, and businessmen. They named their club the African Association. Its stated purpose—"Promoting the Discovery of the Inland

Parts of that Quarter of the world." They intended to resolve once and for all the two geographical mysteries of the Western world: Was there or was there not an opulent metropolis across the peach-colored dunes, and in what direction did this damn Niger River flow?

They would send their own expedition to Africa. They'd all pitch in to pay for it. All they needed was one brave explorer.

Maps were spread across the kitchen table and I was eating a sandwich as I alternated between reading *Qajaq*, an anthropological history of the design of kayaks, which I liked, and Graham Greene's *Journey Without Maps*, which I found disappointing, when Rick Smith stopped by.

Rick was the local itinerant philosopher-carpenter. He wore a maroon beret and a bushy mustache and did remodeling work for friends. He rode his bicycle to their houses and charged them only for the time he worked not the time he spent drinking coffee and talking. It took him six months to do a six-week job. He said it was because "the potential is always greater than the reality." But he did clean, beautiful work and people were willing to put up with the wait.

Rick and I were good friends. Whenever I had the time—he always had the time—we'd throw away an hour or two on art or existentialism. He was in the habit of coming round at lunchtime. Sue didn't mind. She gave him a hug, fixed him a sandwich, heaped chips on the plate, and poured him a large glass of milk.

Rick ate half the sandwich before lifting his plate and examining the maps underneath.

"So. Africa this time."

"Mike and I. Sort of an anniversary adventure."

One thing led to another and naturally he didn't have anything planned and going off to Africa sounded great and he'd been thinking about it himself anyway.

"I'll ask Mike."

Mike didn't know Rick very well. Only that he used to be a swimmer, which counted for something.

"It could make it safer."

"How, Mike? Three's a liability."

"Rick would have to choose a partner."

"Doubles the number of potential accidents."

"Also doubles the number of people who can help out if something gets to be a little too much fun."

This didn't sound like Mike; it sounded like Diana.

Rick was delighted; for years he had been talking about leaving. He had problems with America. All the cardriving and tvwatching and moneymaking got to him. He'd been talking about finding a village somewhere where humans were human and had more time for human things—playing music, talking, hanging out. He was originally going to be a sculptor not a carpenter. This trip was his chance. He said if he found a village along the Niger that he liked, he'd just get himself a mud hut and stay.

Rick chose John Haines as his partner. He and John had once done a bike ride in Tibet together. Like the rest of us, John was from Laramie, but he now lived in Portland. He was a banker. His father had been a banker, as had his grandfather. He was also an environmentalist, an activist. Rick said John was breaking up with his girlfriend and quitting his job. He'd been with both for years. When I talked to him on the phone, he said he saw this trip as an opportunity to stop being a banker and become something closer to what he really was.

That was the team then. Mike, Rick, John, and I. The Niger River Expedition. For our letterhead Rick made a pen-and-ink sketch of a kayaker calmly paddling around a roaring hippo.

Mike and I were primarily interested in running what had never been run, the headwaters. We figured that was about all we'd have time for. Rick and John wanted to do the whole river, source to sea. We had different objectives but that was normal for an expedition.

When you first start doing long trips with other people,

you naively believe everyone shares common goals, your goals. Never. On every expedition each person has entirely personal, often inscrutable hopes and ambitions. That's why no trips work out the way they're planned.

Our first job was to divvy up the task of getting the gear. For certain journeys you go with what you've got—slip on a knapsack and walk out the door. These are often the best adventures and they should be undertaken in no other way. Unfortunately, attempting the first descent of a river is not such a trip. Here is a partial list of the gear we needed:

Foldable kayaks, spray skirts, kayak parts, kayak paddles, canoe paddles, sail, mast, sail parts, life jackets, bilge pumps, throwlines, towlines, water filters, tents, sleeping bags, sleeping pads, stoves, stove parts, fuel bottles, fuel, backpacks, daypacks, dry bags, duffel bags, plastic bags, camp utensils, tarps, topo maps, road maps, geologic maps, medical kit, repair kit, phrase books, bug dope, bug hats, sun dope, sun hats, and a hundred other items you only know you need when you get there and can't get them.

The workload was divided evenly. It was to be a team effort, each of us responsible for procuring some small things and some big things.

As we had done in the past, Mike and I were hoping to persuade a few companies to help finance the trip. It's an old and honorable tradition. Find somebody who has more money than you but less time and then try to convince them that what you're up to is so grand and daring that they really cannot not be a part of it. Columbus did this. Richard Burton. Livingstone. Amundsen. All those guys.

John was wary. Rick proclaimed an ethical aversion to the idea. "It's like prostitution."

For me and Mike sponsorship had always been a means to an end. We gave a company pics of the trip; they gave us their products. Straight business deal. It's how we had managed to do twenty expeditions between us. The gear itself was immaterial. One year it was ice axes and ropes; another, bicycles and panniers; this year, kayaks and paddles—they were all just tools of the trade, no different from a carpenter's level or a plumber's pipe wrench. The journey is what mattered.

Rick and John fretted. They thought such an arrangement might compromise their trip.

"And what trip is that?"

"What are you talking about? Kayaking down the Niger!"

"And where's your kayak? And your plane ticket? And your tent?"

It was quite simple. None of us had the gear we needed to run the Niger, or the money to buy it. We either got sponsorship, or didn't go.

John managed to bring in kayak paddles and a few maps; Mike and I did the rest. From spanking-new $3,500 collapsible sea kayaks to backpacks to boots. Rick didn't even fill out his own visa applications. Sue did it for him, at two in the morning, leaning uncomfortably over the kitchen table, shaking her head and forging his signature.

When the boats arrived, Mike and I immediately put ours together and hauled them out to the Little Laramie River. Mike was still up to speed but I hadn't been boating for a decade. I started with basic paddle work—power stroke, sweep stroke, reverse sweep stroke, J stroke, low brace, high brace. Mike went straight for the roll, nonchalantly flipping over and then snapping himself back up. We went out a half-dozen times to practice.

I think John also got in the water before we left, but unlike the rest of us, he was a kayaker. That's how he described himself. He said kayaking was his sport. He said he'd been boating regularly, so Mike and I assumed he was already ready.

I don't think Rick even took his boat out of the bag. The closest he came to a roll was a big cinnamon one at the coffee shop.

A month after I first called Mike, on 9 October 1991, we left.

Sue and Diana were six months pregnant. They said they would do things together. They said they weren't worried; they knew we would take care of each other.

Sue even told me she would understand if I wasn't back for the birth, although she was lying. She wrote love notes to me in my journal that I would discover weeks later. I bought her a TV. We hadn't had one for years. I thought it might help her relax as her body became uncomfortable.

We walked down the airport causeway holding hands and wiping each other's noses and laughing. Just before I passed through the gate, she grabbed my hands and placed them on her stomach and held them there, looking up at me, trying to smile, whispering that she would kill me if I got myself killed.

SOURCES

School made John Ledyard squirm. He would stare out the window and dream. Four months at Dartmouth and he slipped away. Ran for the woods and took up with the Indians. Lived with them, ate with them, slept beside their campfires, learned to paddle their slim boats on their hidden rivers.

Then one morning he reappeared, his body leaner, his skin ruddier. The Reverend Eleazar Wheelock, founder and proctor of the college, had hoped to turn the young man into an Indian missionary but the apostasy had gone the other way. Ledyard axed down a tree along the Connecticut River, carved himself a dugout, and paddled off.

He showed up in Plymouth, England, four years later. It was 1776, the year Jefferson was drafting the Declaration of Independence. Ledyard had heard that Captain James Cook was planning a third expedition. Being a young man unencumbered by the yoke of rank or protocol, he presented himself before Cook and the captain took him on at once.

They sailed in July. The *Resolution* and the *Discovery*. Cook's mission: to find the fabled Northwest Passage. Two years later, at Unalaska Island, midway in the Aleutian chain, they discovered evidence of white civilization— Indians wearing blue linen shirts and carrying European knives. Ledyard volunteered as a scout. Weaponless, with just a bottle of brandy and a hunk of bread, he allowed the

Indians to stow him inside a kayak. They took him to their camp where he found thirty Russians. They had been there for five years, buying pelts from the Indians.

Still in search of a course through the continent, Cook navigated into the Bering Sea but was stymied by ice. The expedition made its way back to Hawaii where, in a skirmish with islanders, Cook was stabbed in the back, butchered, boiled, and eaten.

On the return voyage Ledyard wrote a book about his travels, *A Journal of Captain Cook's Last Voyage*. He explored at length the similarities between the Indians of the Northwest and those he had lived with in New England. He also compared and contrasted the geographical distribution of plants, animals, customs, and dialects, concluding that the native populations originated either from South America—"the trade winds strongly intimate from that continent"—or from Asia, noting that breadfruit is "nowhere known but among these islands and the islands further northward on the coast of Asia."

After an absence of four years the expedition docked in England. While he was gone, Ledyard had become the citizen of a new nation. He thus became the first American to have seen the Bering Strait, the Pacific coast of Russia, China, the South Pacific, Africa, and Antarctica. But it was the Northwest that captured him. Its grandeur and magnificence were stitched across his soul like the Polynesian tattoos on his hands. He was convinced the Northwest should be part of the United States.

Ledyard returned to his breech-born country and tried to interest merchants in sending a ship to the Northwest. None had the money or the inclination—the country was still recovering from the war. Dismayed, he sailed for England, then on to Paris.

He was penniless but gallant and the Marquis de Lafayette introduced him to the second American minister to France, Thomas Jefferson. Ledyard exchanged ideas for dinner. His enthusiasm was boundless. He insisted on the limitless potential of the Northwest. One candlelit night a

plan was born. He would make a round-the-world recon-
naissance: cross Europe, cross the breadth of Siberia to the
Sea of Okhotsk, take a Russian vessel to the Northwest,
walk across the breadth of North America, then head on
down to Virginia where, by that time, the minister would be
back home awaiting a full report.

No one had ever attempted such a thing. With a small
loan from Jefferson, Ledyard went shopping in Paris. He
bought what he thought he would need for such a journey—
a hatchet, an Indian peace pipe, and two hunting dogs—and
set out.

That winter, 1786–87, the Gulf of Bothnia, between
Sweden and Finland, did not freeze solid. The horse-drawn
sledges that normally traversed the ice weren't running.
Undaunted, Ledyard struck off north. It was dark twenty-
two hours a day. The villages were buried up to their
rooftops in snow. Seven weeks later he stomped into St.
Petersburg with "but two shirts and still more shirts than
shillings." He then drove a set of "wild tartar horses" across
three thousand miles of Siberia before holing up for the
winter in Yakutsk.

Again he pursued his observations, this time recording the
similarities between North American Indians and Siberian
"Tartars." He compared everything from sled dogs to
marriage rituals, yurts to kayaks. In a letter to Jefferson he
wrote, "I am certain that all the people you call red people
on the continent of America, and on the continents of
Europe, and Asia, as far south as the southern parts of
China, are all one people . . . I am satisfied that America was
peopled from Asia, and had some, if not all, its animals from
thence." Furthermore, he continued, "when the history of
Asia, and I add of America, because there is an intimate
connection between them, shall be as well known as that of
Europe, it will be found that those who have written the
history of man, have begun at the wrong end."

Then, in the spring of 1788, he was arrested as a French spy. It was a pretext. Word of American designs on the Russian fur trade in the Northwest had reached Catherine the Great. Just six hundred miles from the Pacific, he was dragged all the way back to Poland. With only the coat he had "slept in, ate in, drank in, fought in and negotiated in," he made his way back to London and looked up an old acquaintance, another veteran of the Cook voyages, Sir Joseph Banks.

Banks at once introduced John Ledyard to Henry Beaufoy, the African Association's secretary. Beaufoy was struck by "the manliness of his person, the breadth of his chest, the openness of his countenance, and the inquietude of his eye. I spread the map of Africa before him."

Beaufoy drew a line across the middle of the continent, from the Red Sea to the Atlantic Ocean. It was a region four thousand miles wide and two thousand miles deep. All of it unknown. Ledyard thought himself "singularly fortunate to be entrusted with the Adventure."

When could he be ready?

"Tomorrow morning."

In August 1788, less than two months after returning from his ordeal in Siberia, Ledyard left England, saying to Beaufoy, "I am accustomed to hardships. I have known both hunger and nakedness to the utmost extremity of human suffering. . . . Such evils are terrible to bear; but they never yet had power to turn me from my purpose. If I live, I will faithfully perform, in its utmost extent, my engagement to the society; and if I perish in the attempt, my honor will still be safe, for death cancels all bonds."

The African Association was elated. The club was a mere three months old and already they had their first explorer. They had high hopes he would set a precedent, and he would.

John Ledyard landed in Alexandria and boated up the Nile to Cairo. From there he intended to strike out overland. After three months he developed liver problems, what he described as a "bilious complaint." The acid of vitriol he took as a remedy burned his insides so severely he resorted to a powerful emetic, and died, vomiting blood.

In 1801, Thomas Jefferson became the third President of the United States. He was a meticulous, perspicacious architect and immediately drew up blueprints for an expedition to the Northwest.

At the time, the western boundary of the United States was the Mississippi River. France owned Louisiana—all land from the Mississippi to the Rockies. In 1803, Jefferson persuaded Napoleon to sell this property, and at a stroke, doubled the size of his fledgling nation.

The next year he sent out two tough chaps to take the rest. Meriwether Lewis and William Clark, with the help of Indian guides, paddled up the Mississippi to its source, crossed the Rockies, ran the Columbia out to the Pacific Ocean, and laid America's claim to the breadth of an entire continent. Sea to shining sea. No matter the Indians.

It is the small creatures that cripple and kill in Africa. The storybooks lie. Lions and leopards are insignificant. Viruses, amoebas, insects, worms, bullets, these are the predators of Africa.

Take blackflies. Common as dirt. Snapping clouds of them vexing skeletal cattle, cloaks of them hanging on hooked meat. They are the dark flowers at the tear ducts of sick children. They lay their eggs in the foam of swift rivers or, if possible, in the arms and legs of people who live beside such water. A worm develops under the flesh and, in time, burrows all the way to the eyeballs, where it dies, taking with it the sight of the human. Scar tissue forms over the pupils and turns them white. It is common in West Africa. It is called onchocerciasis. River blindness.

Slow rivers are no safer. Snails live in them and blood flukes live in the snails. The Nile, for example, is a perfect habitat. The fluke bores painlessly through the skin, shoves off in the nearest bloodstream, boats down to the bowels, and makes camp in the intestines or bladder. Victims find their strength and cheerfulness draining away. They find blood in their piss and shit. This disease is called bilharzia. In the worst case the fluke devours the liver, a mortal bilious disorder.

Most diseases in Africa have metaphorical journeys. Sleeping sickness, trypanosomiasis, is transmitted by the tsetse fly. Typhus is transmitted by ticks. Malaria, the ancient mass murderer of Africa that deftly kills a million people a year, is transmitted by the mosquito. So is yellow fever. AIDS is a mere virus that is annihilating entire countries.

Still, you don't hear that much about any of them. They are too common. Many Africans have one or another of these infirmities and they live with them, don't whine, and die quietly. Insalubrity is a natural state. An undiseased body, without wounds or worms or parasites, is what is unnatural.

What you hear about, of course, are the attacks by the larger assassins, lions or leopards. They aren't any more courageous—they also take the young, the weak, or the ill. But because their ferocity is so rare and so dramatic, it makes for better stories. Even the Africans think so.

The only other exceptions to the tyranny of the minuscule are crocodiles and hippos. Humans need water, so African villages are often along rivers, and tragedies happen.

The woman from the Guinean embassy was right about hippos. They kill as many people as do the big cats—mostly folks plying small boats on muddy rivers. They aren't carnivorous, just territorial. Cross some unidentifiable borderline and hippos charge. Weighing four tons, with a mouth larger than that of any animal other than the whale, they impale you on their tusks, thrash you about like a rag doll, then spit you out.

Crocodiles, on the other hand, eat meat. Spring from beneath green water, snatch whoever is nearby, often children, hold them under until they're drowned, stuff them into some underwater cave, and devour them at their leisure.

The death toll from both hippos and crocs paled immeasurably compared to that of the cunning mosquito, but they did make Mike and me think. We had drugs for the mosquito.

We showed Rick and John photos of a hippo attacking a dugout, snapping it in half, tiny-looking men splashing in brown water. Perhaps, we suggested, we should bring guns.

"That's ridiculous!"

Mike and I weren't convinced either. We'd never taken weapons on an expedition before, never even considered it. Neither of us had ever owned a handgun. The NRA sickened us. But then we didn't live in the jungles of America. We lived in a town where people didn't lock their doors.

There were only two scenarios that warranted bringing a weapon: defending yourself against man, or against beast. To Rick and John, both were preposterous.

"You can't kill a hippo with a gun!"

"Don't have to kill it, just stop it."

We agreed that it could be difficult to halt a charging hippo with a handgun. Or a grim-grinned crocodile, gliding in quiet and fatal as a torpedo. But it had been done. You needed calm aim and a powerful weapon.

Rick and John were upset. They believed in an animal kingdom. Lamb snuggled next to lion. Predators killing only for survival. They didn't believe in guns, neither their purpose nor their efficacy.

As for two-legged predators, they found this possibility even more far-fetched. What kind of person would attack an innocent human being? To them our concerns were insulting. A reflection on us, not mankind.

All four of us had been raised in the same small town in the American West, where it was quite possible, expected in fact, to grow up believing the world was basically good.

35

Which you could do if the atrocities that are happening every second of every day since the beginning of time had not happened to you or your family or the people you love. This is the faith of the lucky. But if just once something terrible happens and you or someone you love becomes unlucky, that faith evaporates. After that you don't look at the world quite the same way. You know something you never wanted to know. You start looking over your shoulder. You don't want whatever happened to happen again. You don't like it but you have to kind of hope yourself into thinking the world is a good place. That only works for a while. Eventually it is necessary to forget about what the world is or is not and just try to hold on to the good things.

Rick and John held fast to homilies about violence. Carry a gun and you'll wind up using it. Go looking for a fight and you'll find one. Better to turn the other cheek.

For me and Mike life was messier than this. We had both lived in Africa. Mike had worked in Swaziland for three years. A small house in a small village laboring at small business development. I'd worked in East Africa as a stringer, a word mercenary. *Time*, AP, Voice of America, *Washington Post*. Anybody who would buy a story or give me an assignment. I'd lived in the flophouses on Latema Street, downtown Nairobi, and slept with an ice ax under my bed.

"We never needed a gun before, Mike."

"Wrong. And you know it. We never had a gun before."

We despised ourselves for our distrust of our fellow man. We worked through ambiguous, hypothetical scenarios. Thieves with families to feed. Desperate young men who needed what we had more than we did.

"They can have it," said Mike. "Possessions are meaningless. That's not what we're talking about. We're talking about life-or-death situations."

We retold and in the process relived the times we had been attacked. Men with knives in Yugoslavia. Men with clubs in South Africa. Men with guns in Siberia. This made us think about our own wives and our unborn children and our families and what their lives would be like without us.

We chose 9-millimeter Rugers and practiced out in the prairie. Set up plastic jugs full of water and blasted away. A 9-millimeter is a large handgun. Ours held clips of seven bullets. One slug would easily kill a human; it might take the whole clip to faze a hippo. It would have been good to practice on moving targets but we left for Africa before we got the chance.

Rick and John were offended.

"We're not in on this. You put them in your bags."

We understood. We'd already made a more difficult decision. When you think it through to the end, to bring a gun is an act of profound selfishness. You are acknowledging that if push comes to shove, you believe your life is more important than another life—and you are willing to kill to keep it.

It is storming the night we arrive in Conakry, Guinea. Rain dark as used motor oil pouring from the sky, the hangar roaring. When lightning explodes, purple then green, macabre snapshots float before our eyes. Negatives of struggling people with their mouths open.

The four of us stand in line and try to look innocent. Mike and I peer around the men with machine guns and past the officer scowling at the faces in the passports then lifting his brutal head and scowling at the owners of the faces. These men don't matter. We're watching the men with pistols in black holsters poking through people's bags.

We hid the guns with our kayaks. Duct-taped them to the aluminum rudders, wrapped foam around the rudders, rolled them up in the kayak skins and placed the bundles in the middle of the bags surrounded by the metal bones of our boats. We are hoping, somehow, an airport X-ray machine will miss them.

We don't see any X-ray machines but sweat is dripping down our ribs anyway. Passenger after passenger is repacking his or her belongings and disappearing through the gates. Our visas are checked. Our passports stamped. The man in front of us is closing up his suitcase. The soldiers are motioning us forward, staring into our eyes looking for fear or guile or any excuse to use their power. Then George Mnabn appears.

George Mnabn is a Guinean living in Germany going home for vacation. We sat beside him on the plane. We didn't tell him about the guns but we did show him our letter from the chargé d'affaires of the embassy of Guinea. It is in French on embossed stationery. It says that Guinea's ambassador to the United States welcomes us to his country and that his countrymen should treat us right. Mike and I had managed to inveigle such a letter from all the ambassadors of the Niger River nations.

Mnabn snatches the paper from Mike's hand and waves it in the faces of the customs officials, yelling at them in their own language. They examine the piece of paper, touch the stamped insignia.

In Western civilization words on pieces of paper are sacred. They have more meaning than a man's handshake or a woman's love. In Africa it's not so simple. Sometimes pieces of paper matter very much, and can save your life, and sometimes they mean nothing—there's no general rule. Usually it's better to have paper than not. Just another card up your sleeve.

The customs officials let us pass. Not one bag is opened. If they had opened our bags and discovered the guns, they would have also found another letter from the chargé d'affaires, on a reasonable facsimile of the original stationery, in French, specifically giving us permission to enter the country with two 9-millimeter Ruger handguns and forty rounds of ammo. Sometimes a bluff is as good as the real thing.

Past the gates George Mnabn shakes our hands and disappears into the arms of his family. We disappear into the claws of two taxi drivers. We are soaked in seconds loading our fifteen bags atop their two Peugeot *quatre-cent-quatres*. They fly us into town with their headlights off, racing each other down slick black streets, playing chicken with the oncoming headlightless vehicles. They know nothing about us except that we don't know the correct fare and that they therefore stand to make some dough. And yet, of all the hundreds of seedy no-name hostels hidden in the squalor of Conakry, they take us to one named The Niger Hotel. Destiny is the coincidence of the random with the inevitable.

Whitewashed walls, high ceilings with fans that work when they feel like it, swaybacked beds, brokentiled showers with fearless cockroaches the size of mice. Rick and John take one room, Mike and I another. After moving our mountain of gear into our rooms, we drink a few warm sour beers. John discovers that someone stole his watch right off his wrist. Must have happened at the airport. He might see it as a good omen, a banker shedding his skin; I don't know.

We have just pulled off our boots and fallen onto the beds when our self-appointed escorts arrive. The door is open and they strut right in. They are young and voluptuous, long thick dreadlocks, ebony skin. They are playful. Perhaps they are surprised we're not old fat men. They flop on to our beds as if they are their own.

They are fluent girls. English, French, several African tongues. When we tell them of our plan, they laugh gaily and say they are more than willing to help us find the source of our raging river, but they want to go dancing first. They want us to take them dancing. Someplace nice. We're beat. Two days straight of flying and layovers and shuttling heavy bags and sitting-up sleep that is not sleep. We try to get rid of them but nothing doing. They're insistent.

It is a cultural experience. A fervid shadowy disco, smooth young bodies sweating and gyrating in unison. We can't dance like they can. We dance like white guys.

The rain has stopped by the time we get out. I try side-stepping the puddles but slip into them anyway. We have no idea where we are. The girls lead us back to our hotel, following us up the steps. In the hallway we thank them for the dancing. They don't understand. John and Rick disappear into their room and shut the door.

"This is your department, isn't it." Mike grins, opens our

door and heads for the bathroom. He didn't want to go out in the first place. He didn't come here for the cultural experience. Mike came to boat.

I am exhausted and drunk and gently push them out and reel onto the bed.

I'm up early the next morning. Everyone else is asleep. I close the door quietly and turn around and she is standing there, Patricia, the most beautiful of last night's courtesans. She is staring out the window down into the street, her bare elbows on the rough windowsill. She lets me look at what I have missed for a moment, then pirouettes.

"Good morning, Mark."

"Good morning, Patricia."

"*Tu as bien dormi?*" she asks, wanting to know if I slept well.

"Yes, I did. But did you?"

"Yes, thank you." She smiles coyly.

I don't understand what she is doing here. I thought our lack of intentions was clear last night.

"You know I can help you." Her body is lithe, mellifluous, her eyes the color of agate. I can see her dark breasts beneath her blouse.

"Perhaps, but no thank you."

"You want to find the source of your river, right?" She touches my waist. Her eyes move. She is teasing me. She knows she is making me uncomfortable.

"No. Thank you, but no."

Suddenly she starts laughing, her teeth shining, her head shaking and rattling the beads in her hair.

"Well then, you must go to the river first. You must start in the middle, then go back to the beginning."

"What?" I am nonplussed.

"You guys must go to Faranah. The Niger is at Faranah."

"I know. I know that."

"Ah, but *tu ne connais pas la route.*"

"We can find it."

She smiles at me. "I will show you."

That is apparently the end of discussion. She unsnaps her purse, withdraws a small white package, and sets it on the windowsill. She opens it delicately, as if she were opening a flower. Inside are two French pastries. She pinches one between her thumb and fingers and raises it. I put out my hand, palm up. She passes the pastry slowly over my hand, pushes the corner of it into my mouth, and licks her long fingers.

"*Bon appétit*, Mark."

When Rick wakes up, Patricia walks us to an obscure bus stop several blocks away. We wait for the right bus. She knows which one. She pays her own fare. The bus winds through the dense tangles of Conakry out to an open-air transportation terminal. There are hundreds of battered buses full but not moving with people hanging out the windows and huge cargo trucks with wheels being changed and taxis sliding away honking or parked with hawkers standing on the hoods shouting.

Rick tells Patricia we want to take a bus to Faranah.

"No, you must take a taxi."

We think she thinks we are wealthy.

"Patricia," says Rick, "all Americans are not rich."

"Yes, actually, they are."

Rick and I check bus after bus while she waits in the shade. It is hot and dusty. We are told the same thing again and again. Deriss no bass to farrana. Eventually a bus driver gets fed up. *No bass! Okay?*

Patricia haggles with the taxi driver. Her beauty stuns him. She knows what it should cost. She explains to him where our hotel is and that he should be there at eight A.M. sharp.

In the morning I don't expect the taxi driver to be there, but he is. So is Patricia. She watches us load our bags on top of the taxi and tie them down with ropes. The weight of our gear bows the roof in. When we are ready to leave, I turn to her and shake her hand.

"Patricia. Thank you."

She looks away.

When she first came to our hotel room, her eyes had probed me so intimately I was the one who had turned my head.

She speaks without looking at me.

"I cannot go with you Mark?"

"No."

"I would like to. I would like to go away. *M'échapper*."

As we roll off, she waves once, then stands with her arms at her sides as if she were lashed to the street.

We blast through town, the horn blaring, the driver swerving madly around potholes, chickens, children, sheep. I am in the front seat beside the driver, Mike and Rick and John are in the backseat. Mike already has his eyes closed. He can sleep anywhere, in any position, at any time. Rick and John are white-knuckled, jerking at each close call.

African cabbies are frustrated race car drivers. They drive their clattertraps as fast as they will go. If you don't like it, there are three things you can do. Asking the driver to slow down is not one of them. He will take it as an insult, as proof that you are another arrogant foreigner who thinks he knows everything, and drive even faster.

One. You can make the driver stop, take down your bags, and leave you alongside the road where you can wait for the next driver who knows you are stuck and hence will stick you himself, charging tenfold.

Two. You can worry yourself sick, imagining yourself dead by beheading, or paralyzed, or your limbs severed into chunks.

Three. You can forget about it, putting your trust in pure luck.

Traveling in developing countries you go through a natural progression. You try the first two several times before you get to the last one and can relax.

Not far outside the city we are stopped by military police. A soldier waves us to the side of the road. Another soldier leans into the driver's window. He is pleased to find us inside. We are asked to get out of the car and show our passports and visas. We do this while the first soldier circles the load on top of the taxi, prodding it with the barrel of his rifle.

When the soldiers start fucking with us, commanding us to undo the ropes and drag down our bags, Mike produces our letter from the embassy. He had held off, hoping it wouldn't be necessary, but obviously the soldiers are too bored to pass up four white foreigners.

They look at the letter. We can't tell if they can read or not. We don't think so. They decide we can go but that they will keep the letter. Rick and John get back into the taxi. Mike steps forward until his face is six inches from the face of the soldier folding up the letter.

"We are not leaving without our letter." His voice is calm and hard.

He is calling their bluff. It surprises them. They had hoped to make a scene, out here on the road where no one would know, but they sure as hell didn't want it to turn into an international incident.

In the next eight hours we will be stopped five more times. We don't get out again. Mike and I talk about it and decide we aren't going to play their game. We put on our sunglasses and hold our paper out the window. It delights our driver. Each time he laughs and slaps the steering wheel and stomps the gas pedal.

When we get into the mountains, it starts to rain, then pour. Soon it's coming down so hard it's as if we are driving underwater, the windshield opaque with streaming liquid. The driver doesn't even think of slowing down.

I crack the steaming window and stick out my hand. My right shoulder and leg become soaked instantly, but I want to feel the rain. When you're from a place so high and cold that even in the summer everything dropping out of the sky is ice, warm rain is shockingly sensual.

I roll up the window, put my head back, and let my eyes go blank staring at the wipers sweeping hypnotically back and forth, back and forth.

There was a girl with eyes shaped like teardrops across the aisle from me. I was trying to talk to her but she only stared.

"She likes you."

"She hasn't said a word, Mike."

"Well she's smiling like anything."

"Now how can you tell?"

Her mother was seated beside her eating dates, her hand disappearing beneath the black veil, then dropping down into a plastic bag on her lap, then disappearing again. She had a tattoo of blue dots on her forehead.

"What. Is. Your. Name?"

The girl wasn't listening. Her eyes were watching my lips.

I pointed to myself and gave my name.

She didn't follow my hand. She was watching my mouth. I looked away and asked her where she was going.

"Casablanca? Marrakesh?"

She was still watching my mouth.

I became self-conscious. I licked my lips. No girl had ever watched my mouth. I didn't know what to do. My pants suddenly felt tight.

"Somethin', isn't it." Mike was leaning forward staring at her. I felt my face go red and he turned back toward the window.

When I glanced over at her again, she had her hand up under her blouse. She was arching her back. I knew I shouldn't look. I knew I should look away but I couldn't. She knew I was watching. For the first time she looked me in the eyes. Her eyelashes and her eyebrows and her eyes were jet-black.

She brought a flat brown bottle out from under her blouse.

Her mother was regarding the bus. It was filled with hazy

blue smoke from the old men smoking hash. The young men had pulled down their pointed hoods. The eyes of the women were shut inside their slits like old soldiers. The mother searched up inside her clothes and brought out another flat bottle and slipped it to her daughter.

The girl tried to give us the bottles.

Mike looked at me. "What'd you do?"

"Nothin'."

"Yeah right. She's just doing this out of the blue."

We had no idea what was going on. This was our first bus ride in Africa. We had tried to hitchhike south from Tangier. Spent a day and a half tramping along the road with our thumbs out. People yelled at us, one guy threw a soda bottle that exploded at our feet, no one stopped. We boarded a bus bound for Marrakesh in the next village.

She was holding the bottles across the aisle with her sleeves partially concealing them, her eyes flitting about the bus.

Mike read the labels.

"Whiskey?"

"How should I know."

Her whisper burned us. We each took a bottle.

"What's she doing?"

She was making desperate motions with her arms.

"She wants us to hide them."

"Forget this." Mike crossed over me and tried to give his bottle back but she wouldn't take it.

The bus was starting to slow down and the girl became frantic. Suddenly she reached across the aisle, lifted up my shirt, snatched the bottle from my hand and pushed it down inside my pants.

"What the hell's going on!"

The bus had stopped. The doors were opening. Soldiers boarded the bus and began shouting, making people stand up, poking their rifles into the bags on the racks and on the floor.

When they got to our row one of the soldiers lowered the point of his rifle against the stomach of the mother and

45

pushed gently. She laughed. She held up her bag of dates and offered him some. The soldier turned to us. He eyed us one at a time, slowly moving his head. Then he spat a seed at us and moved on. The soldier behind him flicked my cap.

The soldiers took their time making people open their jackets and their boxes. They laughed a lot. Eventually they got off the bus, the last one wagging his rifle at the bus driver before jumping out the door crowing.

When the bus was moving again, we yanked the bottles out of our pants and tried to give them back. The girl and her mother wouldn't touch them. Other passengers on the bus were watching us. I thought they didn't understand what had just happened. They were angry at *us*, not at the girl and her mother. We tried to put the bottles back in the mother's lap but a large man in a gray djellaba and a knife in his belt came down the aisle and removed the bottles from her and gave them back to us.

We sat back. The mother took a chocolate bar from her bag on the floor, unwrapped it, and gave it to us. At first we tried to refuse it but then we gave in. The girl peeled each of us an orange. She passed us the small globes; then her hands disappeared under her veil. I could hear her. She was licking her fingers.

She watched me eat the orange. I should have been angry or at least acted like I was, but she was watching my mouth eat the orange.

The next time soldiers searched the bus, after they got off and we were moving again, Mike said, "Let's just throw them out the window." He tried to open his window. It was stuck and he started pounding on it.

The mother began talking nervously to the hook-nosed men in the seat in front of her.

I whispered at Mike under my breath.

It was an eleven-hour bus ride. The mother and the girl fed us. We knew we were pathetic. We loathed ourselves but we didn't have the courage just to give back the whiskey and get off the bus. We talked about it but we thought someone might set us up, or turn us in as smugglers, or stab us.

Besides that, we wouldn't get full use of our two-dollar bus ticket.

The chocolate melted on my fingers and I had to lick them and the girl watched. She never tired of her duty. She watched my lips, making me believe things would happen that I knew could never happen.

The last time soldiers searched the bus one of them made me and Mike stand up. Our shirttails were out and he was staring at us and I couldn't believe he didn't see the bulges in our pants. He grinned. He kept grinning. I was sure he had figured it out and was about to ram the butt of his rifle into our groins shattering the bottles.

The next time the bus stopped, the mother and her daughter stood up and gathered their belongings amid the spillings of orange scraps and chocolate wrappers. The girl spoke to us. She was asking for the bottles back but we pretended we didn't understand. She put out her hand.

Mike was incensed. "After we about got ourselves killed for it!"

Everyone in the bus was staring, waiting to see what would happen, knowing it could only happen one way. Even the bus driver was peering at us, one eye in the wedge of unbroken mirror.

"This is crazy!" Mike handed her his bottle and she gave it to her mother.

I didn't move so she lifted my shirt and put her hand in my pants. I felt her fingernails against my abdomen. She handed the bottle to her mother and the old woman wobbled off the bus. But the girl didn't follow her. She moved forward and closed her legs around my knees.

The sun was low now, coming red through the narcotic smoke. From under her blouse she produced a small vial with a silver cap. She bent over me, took my hand and formed it into a cup. I looked up. I couldn't see her eyes now, her veil hung in the way. For the first time I saw her lips, her red mouth. She unscrewed the cap and placed it between her lips. Her tongue came out. She slipped her fingers into her mouth and delicately put the cap on the end of her tongue.

47

Leaning closer, she tipped the vial. Perfume streamed into my palm, liquid cool and clear and smelling of lilacs.

We reach Faranah at dusk. Flat hills of bluebrown chaparral. We have a name, John Olafson. Acquaintance of an acquaintance like so many people one searches out when traveling. A Swede working for a Norwegian firm contracted to string telecom lines across Guinea.

The driver drops us and our pile of duffels outside the gates of the compound. The guard is like a friendly dog. He won't let us in, says he can't let us in, then lets us in. We find Olafson and his wife Margot in their sunken living room watching *Nuns on the Run*. They have no idea who we are or what we're doing inside their compound. They invite us in to drink beer and watch the video.

The beer is excellent, the video painful—a fatuous English skit only homesick Europeans could find funny.

Olafson insists we camp inside the compound. We raise our tents on the manicured gravel between the swimming pool and the servants' quarters. We are itching to see the river.

"Where's the Niger?" asks Rick.

"Just down the road." Olafson motions with his head. "Be my guest."

The guard smiles and nods and lets us out and the four of us take a walk in the night. We don't know what the river will look like. We have maps but maps only tell you where something is, not what it is.

The road tilts down to an iron bridge. We step carefully out to the middle and stick our heads through the girders. It is a dark night but we can see the river. It is black. Black as lava and deep and moving fast. We can't see where it is coming from or where it is going.

It is not so good to see a river for the first time in the dark. It is like crawling up a ridge at midnight and facing for the first time a mountain you intend to scale, or a castle you intend to storm. The darkness can shake you. Darkness makes everything monstrous and foreboding. What you cannot see you imagine and what you imagine is more terrible than what exists. There is reason to teach your children not to be afraid of the dark: to overcome the fear of the dark is to overcome the fear of the unknown, which is to overcome fear itself.

When we come off the bridge, someone is speaking to us from a shack on the bluff above the black river. We walk over. A curtain of chickens, claws trussed, necks wagging, hangs across the opening. Underneath is a line of warm Fantas. In between is a shriveled face with leaky eyes.

"Rivah no good."

"Excuse me?" asks John.

"Rivah eat mahn."

"Eat what?"

"Mahn he dispear in rivah."

"When?"

"Two days ago."

"How did it happen?"

"Devul."

We chuckle, but it sounds forced. The old man shakes a hooked finger at us and starts bobbing his head and rocking.

"Devul, devul, devul."

In the morning John asks Olafson who might have fallen in the river and drowned.

"Could've been anyone. Bloody river kills people all the time."

"They don't know how to swim?"

"Some. But they vanish nonetheless. That river's no playground."

He and Margot have already expressed their dismay over our trip. Olafson begins to itemize the dangers while Margot concurs with little nods.

"By God, you'd better watch out for the maggot flies. They incubate in your flesh like larvae, then one day burst out splitting your skin wide open.

"And this Lassa disease. I know you're just in-country but

you've heard about it certainly. Thing's like some kind of black plague. Killed three people already."

Guinea worm, puff adders, water snakes, black mambas, green mambas. It's a wonder there is a human left alive on the continent of Africa.

"Get bit by a green mamba and you're dead. Period. Stiff as a fucking board in three hours. Nothing can save you."

Mike put our medical kit together. He gave us each a three-page printout of what it contained. Later that day Rick and John ask him if he thinks it is complete enough to handle all these contingencies.

"Nope."

They frown gravely.

"We'll just have to improvise. That's part of the fun."

They think he is being sarcastic. He is not. He is being candid. It is impossible to be prepared for everything. For Mike, improvisation is an essential element of adventure.

"Remember, guys," I say, "they're expats."

Like all expats in Africa, the Olafsons don't quite live in Africa. They live inside a walled compound with guards and guard dogs and gardeners, servants and chauffeurs, flush toilets and air conditioning. The Olafsons aren't typical though because they don't whine about it. They openly admit they have chosen exile. They are in Africa to make money, plain and simple. They plan to retire twenty years before everyone else.

Most expats, when they go back to their own country (twice a year, expenses paid), find it too tame and talk ceaselessly of the drama and wildness of their life in Africa. But then back in Africa they take every precaution to make their lives just as they would be if they lived at home—except for the servants and the cases of expensive liquor and the very good money (hardship bonuses and all).

Even foreign correspondents are like this. That's something I learned in East Africa. People have this image of foreign correspondents out there on the edge getting the tough story for the betterment of mankind, but most of them are just expats. They live behind walls of money, drink like fish, and spend all their time with other soused white people. They send their stringers out to get the story.

Of course they have a special excuse. James Wilde, an erstwhile African correspondent for *Time*, explained it to me once.

Wilde was wild. Supposedly related to Oscar, he told me he got his start in journalism by procuring whores for the journalists in Southeast Asia back in the 1940s. Rumor had it that he was once such a hard drinker he had to have his stomach sewn up. I liked him. If he'd done a quarter of what he said he had, he'd been around.

I stopped in at his office one day in Nairobi and there were piles of neatly stacked magazines and newsletters spread across the floor. Each stack was from a different political faction in Africa. Socialists, Communists, anarchists, imperialists, Renamo, Frelimo, Unita, MPLA, ANC, SNM, NPFL, INPFL, EPLF, EPRDF . . . he kept up on all of them.

When I came in, he put down what he was reading.

"Sometimes I forget who's who. They all illustrate their propaganda with messy pictures of the atrocities that they claim their enemy perpetrated upon them."

I didn't know anything about Africa so I couldn't answer.

"You want to know what I think?" He twisted his leathery face. "I think they are all telling the truth . . . and they're all lying." He cackled sourly.

It was the summer of 1987 during the time of the All African Games. President Daniel Arap Moi had banned American journalists from covering the games because Amnesty International had just published a report on Kenya's human rights violations. I'd gotten myself a forged German passport and invented fake letters of invitation and spoke passable German and wanted to cover the games for *Time*. After I made my pitch, Wilde grimaced.

"Let me tell you something. This is the way it works: Americans don't give a *flying fuck* about Africa. They couldn't care less about the African Games. In terms of

Africa's newsworthiness back in the good ole U.S. of A., there's an equation. You want it?"

I nodded.

"The death of five hundred black Africans is equal to the death of fifty white Africans, which is equal to one pretty white coed getting herself gored in the foot by a rhino."

Olafson said he would provide us with a vehicle and his best driver, Thomas Moses. Moses is instructed to take us upriver until the road ends.

"From there," Olafson sighed, "you're on your own to make the best of your own undoing."

We leave at daybreak in an immaculate Land Cruiser. We pass over the bridge, turn right onto a narrow stretch of road slicing through the bush, and don't see the Niger again.

Thomas Moses dodges the deep holes and misses the overhanging limbs and swings up and around the wide puddles. He doesn't talk much. He is a professional. He keeps his eyes on the road, adjusts the AC. After a while he pushes in a Johnny Cash tape.

We don't know where Thomas Moses will leave us or how we will reach the source from there. We don't know where the source is exactly. Our most detailed maps are 1/200,000 Cartes de l'Afrique. Hand-drawn in the 1930s by meticulous French cartographers, the topography is almost unreadable. Instead, the charts are dense with names. Bokonkekonko, Koumbatamba, Mafinnedi Kabaya, Serelinkonko. More enamored with the lilt of Malinke than the lay of the land, the Parisian mapmakers left the course of the greatest river in West Africa indiscernible, its source a secret.

But maps won't help much anyway. The Fouta Djallon is an equatorial mountain range. Mike and I have been in mountains like this before—we know what to expect. There will be no open woods, no clean peaks, no expansive meadows. The Fouta Djallon will be jungle: rumpled geology smothered by the octopus of botany. We will not be able to scramble up a ridge, take bearings, triangulate, reconnoiter, and go. It is impossible to follow a straight line in the jungle. Instead, we will have to take footpaths. Footpaths curl and hook and divide. They are like a maze. No signs, no clues. If you don't already know the way, you can walk in circles until you go mad. There is only one answer. To find the source of the Niger we will need a guide. Our map will be his mind, our compass his intuition.

As we travel south toward the mountains, the terrain changes from brown to green. Acacias and horny scrub-cover are replaced by swales of hip-high grass and chunks of canopied forest. Beyond the towns of Laya Doula and Banian the road diminishes to a rough track and we climb into the foothills.

In the village of Nianforando, Thomas Moses stops to let his engine cool. Dust plumes up around the vehicle as he lifts the hood. The four of us get out and stand in the dirt.

The iron-roofed, cement-block buildings of the flatlands are gone. We stand among beehive huts with conical straw roofs. Women are working. Carrying large baskets on their heads or bundles of firewood or farm implements, their latest infants swaddled to their backs. Men are sitting in the shade. Happy, shyless kids, rolled in red dirt as if in flour, begin to gather around us.

Suddenly, around a mud hut, comes a man on a tall black bike.

He is a stick of a man. He is wearing a brown fedora set squarely on a slender head, a brilliant white shirt, and a dark sport jacket. He is riding with his back ramrod stiff like a man proud to be on a bicycle. He is wheeling straight at us, cutting a line in the dirt, his coattails floating. As he draws close, he stops pumping and presses gently backward on the pedals. Twenty feet out, he leaps from the bike, lands lightly beside it, takes three bounding steps, and halts in front of us.

"Gentlemahns, I am much glad I hahve found you!"

His teeth gleam. His face is so dark and thin it could have been carved from mahogany.

"My name is Sori Keita." He puts out a bony hand.

We each shake his hand and give our names and he repeats them saying each time, "Fery good to meet you, sir."

"And now. How are you coming, gentlemahns? You are getting closer."

We glance at each other.

"You want to go to *Tembakounda*."

"We want to go to the source of the Niger River," says Mike.

"Yes, that is it. Tembakounda."

John asks him if he has been there.

"Yes, of course. That is why I come here. I am your guide."

He states this so matter-of-factly, with such certainty and candor, it draws smiles from all of us.

"You *have* been there."

"I have been there."

"When?"

"Eighteen years ago. For French man with Africa wife."

"You know the way."

"I know the way."

We believe him.

Most of the time in life when you meet people, you have no idea whether they are telling the truth. They might be; they might not be. Their face is a mask. But once in a while you meet someone who you know, instinctively, is telling the truth. Sounds hokey, but it happens.

We ask him how soon he can be ready.

"I say good-bye to wives."

He raises one finger, lifts his bicycle, sets it down in the direction he wants to go, swings on, and pedals away.

We wait no more than five minutes before Sori returns. He comes walking around a hut taking long strides for a little man. He is still in his suit jacket and fedora and cheap plastic sandals. In his right hand is a small gym bag.

"Gentlemahns"—he tips his hat—"let us go."

54

This is the way with all mythical guides. They find you, you don't find them. Their senses are keener than yours. They are like carrier pigeons, or Seeing Eye dogs. They are meant to guide you. You are meant to let them.

From that moment, until we slide our boats into the flickering brown Niger and slip away forever, we are in the hands of Sori Keita.

Beyond Nianforando the track turns to mud and begins to disappear. Sori sits with his little bag on his knees. The jeep lurches and slams and he, a man as light as a boy, remains tranquil and balanced without holding on, as if he were his own ballast.

Sori says the trail will end at the next village. The last two miles are so steep and slick all of us get out and walk. We keep glancing over our shoulders, expecting the jeep to start sliding backward, hitch sideways, and tumble downhill. Or for Thomas Moses to roll down his window and say it is impossible to continue. But he has his dignity. Penetrating the fecund, dripping mountains is a test of his mastery as a driver.

The village at the end of the road is called Bambaya. A collection of twenty beehive huts set in a circle surrounded by jungle. When the jeep grinds up, Sori immediately climbs onto the roof and begins handing down our bags. After the roof is unloaded, Thomas Moses turns his Land Cruiser around and vanishes down the hill without looking back.

We shuttle the bags into the dark cave of a hut. Sori says it is his brother's home. There is a mud bench around the outer wall, a scimitar in a leather sheath hung on a wooden peg, a mattressless iron bed canopied with a ratty bug net and two skins on a dirt floor.

We stack our gear near the entrance. In addition to our individual backpacks, we have nine duffel bags—four containing the collapsible kayaks, five with expedition equipment—and one long cardboard box full of paddles.

55

Bereft of the strength of machines, the pile appears immense.

I ask Sori how far Tembakounda is from here.

"Three days."

"We will need porters."

"Boys with drums coming."

I don't know what he means.

"Men hear drums. Men hear what drums say. Men come."

There isn't a telephone in this village. There are no telephones anywhere we are going. The few attempts at roads have been washed away. Villages still communicate with each other via drums. Sori says the sound of a drum can be heard ten kilometers away. It would take a runner an hour to go that distance. And a runner could only go to one place.

He and I are standing together outside the hut. Mike and Rick and John have gone to look around the village. Sori stretches out his arm and twirls in a circle.

"Drums go all places."

As I stare into the jungle encircling us, he asks me if I have ever been someplace like this.

"No," I say. "Many times."

Sori grins. It is an African answer.

"Then here you will like."

"Already do, Sori."

I am exactly where I want to be. One of the last obscure places. Somewhere not yet crosshatched with highways and bound with wire. Running the Niger is just a good excuse to come here.

Places with no roads and no wires are bigger than other places. Distance hasn't been distorted. People claim the world is getting smaller, as if it were some green and blue balloon leaking air. Africans don't buy this. To most Africans the world is enormous. Why? Because they walk. They have no choice; they are poor. If you must use your own legs—your own blood, bone, and sinew—to travel from one place to another, a mile is a mile and the world is boundless.

Places with no roads and no wires are also more mortal

— S O U R C E S —

than other places. They are so because you cannot escape. Can't fly away or drive away or phone for help. If you want to leave, you must walk. If you cannot walk, you must have the help of those around you—if they will help you. Thus kindnesses are not overlooked, mistakes not forgotten, cowardice not forgiven. In such a place, or on an expedition into such a place, what goes around comes around. Everything boomerangs.

But then mortal places are usually better to visit than to live in. The living is too grievous.

Sori takes us across the commons to meet the chief of the village. The chief is seated on a stool in his hut in the dark, enfolded in orange fabric. He wears wing tips with no socks. Beneath a white skullcap is a face creased in all directions.

Sori explains what we are doing here while the chief looks at us. Sori keeps talking. The chief asks Sori questions but holds his eyes on us. Sori answers. The chief asks more questions. Sori answers. The chief nods and we go out.

The drummers have arrived. Three muscular youths in tattered drawers, each with a different-size drum. One drum is large and fat and untapered; one is bottleneck-shaped; one is narrow and tall. The drums lie on their sides on the ground, their heads facing a small fire. Naked children are springing across the commons adding bouquets of brown grass to the flames. Sori says the drums have skin heads that grow soft from the dampness and have to be dried to become taut.

After a while the drummers begin tuning their instruments, each man searching for a voice only he can recognize. The sounds the drums make are astounding: cracking detonations loud as a firecracker, but deeper, richer. They rumble the jungle.

It is dark now. We go back to our hut and find two platters of food on the floor. Rice and boiled chicken. We sit down and eat in the blackness, our right hands squeezing balls of rice and dipping them into the stew, our chins and fingers dripping grease.

The doorway is crowded with the heads of children. John

57

entertains them by making finger shadows on the mud wall with the aid of his headlamp.

In a little while the isolated reports fired into the jungle stop and the drums begin to sing together. Rick asks Sori what the drums are saying.

"They say come. Come to Bambaya. Strange people here."

"What else can the drums say?"

Sori says the drums can say many, many things, but when they call other villages they say only big things. A birth, a death, a dance. A stranger, a wedding, a fight.

After dinner we leave the hut and return to the commons. The drums have been singing for an hour. A large crowd has gathered. Sori pulls the four of us through the crowd into the circle.

The fire is now a pillar of flames. The drummers stand half-crouched, drums between their knees, backs arched, eyes closed. They are sweating; their bodies glisten. Beside the drummers is the chief, his vast orange robe stained scarlet from the bonfire. Surrounding the fire and the drummers and the chief are perhaps two hundred villagers.

The chief moves out into the open space inside the circle and begins to spin. He holds his arms up and throws his head back and in the leaping red light his figure ripples with shadow and burning.

Sori pulls us close to him.

"I must dance with chief now." The reverberation of the drums is so loud he is yelling. Sori slips from his sport jacket, folds it on my forearm, and moves out toward the chief.

He stretches his arms out like wings. His white shirt glows like an apparition. His skin is so black his hands and head vanish. All we can see is the ghost of a man spinning in circles, arms sweeping back and forth to the heavy beat.

The chief circles Sori and Sori circles the chief and then they meet in the middle like a pair of ancient vultures, one burning white, the other burning red. The villagers clap and sing and the chief and Sori dance together for some time.

Then the sound of the drums abruptly lessens. The roar subsides. The chief glides back to his seat beside the drummers and Sori returns to us. The drumming becomes a throbbing whisper and the chief motions to Sori.

Sori steps back inside the circle and begins speaking to the crowd in their tongue. He points to us. He tells them who we are and where we are going. He says we need men to help carry our equipment. Two dozen men step forward into the firelight. They are from different villages. Sori selects ten of them. He does not choose the big men. He chooses small, wiry men. As he leads them out of the circle, the drums leap up again like the flames and every man, woman, and child spills into the circle dancing.

Sori takes the ten little men to our hut. We follow him. Inside, we shine our headlamps for them and they wander among the huge bags testing each one. Lifting it by the straps, dropping it, lifting another, chattering to themselves.

Earlier we had asked Sori what men were paid for difficult work—humping rice, lumber, straw. He said $1.50 a day. We said we would pay twice that.

Shouting erupts. The men are arguing about something, pushing each other, pointing at the bags. They are lifting the bags higher now and throwing them down. Sori does not intervene. The row ends quickly with five of the ten men exiting the hut. The remaining five turn to Sori and the smallest of them speaks. He says they will come in the morning before light. Sori nods and they file out the hole in the wall.

We are paying by the load, not by the man. Three dollars for transporting one fifty-pound bag up to the next village. The men have just doubled their loads, thereby doubling their pay. I think they are showing off. Double loads are impossible.

Suddenly I realize what is happening. We are being made fools! Duped. It is well documented. Travelers have been fulminating on the character of porters for centuries, invariably describing them as loafers, drunkards, avaricious knaves. The whole thing has been a farce. They'll show up all right, around noon. Then it will start all over. Again they will wander about hefting the bags; soon they will demand more money. Completely dependent upon their assistance, we will argue but acquiesce. Then they'll walk around some more. Feigning straining, barely able to raise one of our duffels off the ground, they will act as if it were an almost impossible task to carry a single load, let alone a double load. Which of course is true. *Fait accompli*, their five brethren will reappear out of the jungle. Eventually, after further negotiations, all ten porters will be loaded and our trek will begin. But by then it will be midafternoon and they will soon strike—stop on the trail and refuse to go further until the ante is once again upped.

And so on for days. That is the way it works with porters. I'd read about it.

The death of Ledyard did not stop the African Association. They already had another man in Africa, Simon Lucas.

Lucas seemed like the ideal candidate. As a youth he had been captured by pirates and sold into slavery in North Africa. After three years of captivity he had been ransomed by England and he became the British vice-consul for Morocco. He spent sixteen years there and became fluent in Arabic. On his return to Great Britain he was appointed oriental interpreter to the Court of St. James.

Lucas shipped across the Mediterranean and arrived in Tripoli as Ledyard was dying in Egypt, October 1788. By sending Ledyard east to west and Lucas north to south, the African Association intended to bring Timbuktu squarely into its crosshairs.

After six months of preparation, Lucas set out on his mission. Rumors of rebel tribesmen turned him around in four days and he scurried back to England.

But there was no lack of volunteers to replace Ledyard and Lucas. It was a time when geographic exploration was an integral part of the pursuit of knowledge. To be an explorer was to be a hero to all men—scholars, politicians, peasants.

In 1790 the African Association selected Major Daniel Houghton as their next explorer. Houghton was a fifty-year-old retired soldier, a hardy, jovial Irishman. He had spent three years posted on the island of Goree off the coast of Senegal and spoke some Malinke. He had a wife, three children, and mountainous debts. He was looking for a job. He would explore Africa if the African Association would take care of his family.

With the eastern and northern approaches rebuffed, the Association sent Major Houghton to the west coast of Africa. He was to boat up the Gambia River then travel eastward overland. His mission was identical to that of his predecessors: to find Timbuktu, find the river Niger.

Houghton followed orders. He arrived on the Gambia in the autumn of 1790. When the river became impassable, he headed inland with a horse and several mules. He escaped ambush after overhearing an old crone describing a plot on his life. In the kingdom of Woolli he lost most of his possessions when a fire razed the village. A rifle exploded in his hands wounding his face and arms. A chief robbed him of the crimson waistcoat he had planned to wear before the king of Timbuktu. His interpreter absconded with his horse and mules. He got malaria.

But Houghton was tough, cheerful, and optimistic. In rags and so sunburned he was often taken for a Moor, he made light of his condition, describing it as a fine disguise— it made him anonymous, and travel through hostile country easier.

In the summer of 1791 the African Association received a letter from Houghton. It came from somewhere deep in Africa, passed hand to hand for a thousand miles, and contained remarkable information. Houghton said the Niger was neither the Senegal River nor the Gambia, but an entirely different watercourse whose source was hidden somewhere in the mountains south of Gambia. Furthermore, the Niger flowed east. This was the first solid information about the enigmatic Niger in two centuries.

Major Daniel Houghton's last note is dated 1 September 1791: "In good health, on my way to Timbuktu, robbed again."

The porters wake us gently, shaking our shoulders. They apologize but they need our help. Just for a minute, then we can go back to sleep.

The air is murky and damp. They have already silently carried all the bags out of the hut, divvied them up, and bound them with cord into five enormous bundles. It takes two of them to get one load up onto a man's head. Three men are already loaded. They stand motionless in the gray dawn, feet together, arms arcing upward to help support the great weight on their heads. Only the muscles in their necks bulge.

They need our help because the two stevedores left cannot load themselves. The men take off their shirts and roll them into snakes and coil them on top of their heads. Then they step forward, spread their legs, put their hands on their thighs, crouch slightly, and curl their toes into the dirt. Mike and I hoist up one load, Rick and John raise the other. The two men straighten up with their chins down, shifting the weight to find the right balance.

Then the five of them take off together, single file, bare-foot, passing deftly through the sleeping village and vanishing into the jungle.

I am stunned. Each load is almost one hundred pounds.

Sori has told them what village to go to, Keressadji. We will get new porters there. These men are hired for one day. Sori says they cannot be gone from their work long.

On the map Keressadji is twelve miles away. But map miles and trail miles are two different things. Whatever the distance is on the map, in the field, after all the wriggling and switchbacking, descending and ascending, it becomes half again as far. Maps only tell half-truths. You have to read between the contour lines.

We leave twenty minutes after the porters, each of us carrying our own pack—a forty-pound load comprising a bag, tent, clothes, camera, food, and water. Sori is wearing a new blue daypack I gave him. He loves it. All the odd contents of his gym bag fit easily inside.

The trail is a wet slit through razor grass and bracken and black trees garroted by vines. Monkeys thrash overhead. Birds screech. It is steep up and then steep down, slipping and grabbing. In the valleys the undergrowth is hacked through with a machete leaving a gauntlet of stalk spikes that stab the soles of our boots. I can't imagine our porters—they're barefoot.

I keep thinking we should catch them any minute. Find them broken, sitting beside the path, their heads between their knees. Maybe they won't even be there and we'll just find our huge duffels abandoned in the mud.

The four of us tramp behind Sori. Sori wants to talk. It is difficult to maintain his cadence and talk. He is never out of breath. He wants to talk about Merica. I am just behind him trying to move as he moves. When he spies me over his shoulder, he grins. He asks me if it is true that people in Merica drive cars to do everything.

"Yes."

"You, Mawk?"

"In town I ride a bicycle."

He asks me if I have ever ridden my bicycle very far, for many days, and I tell him I have.

"I hahve also."

He says he once had a car, when he was a young man, but when it broke down he could not fix it. He says he can fix his bicycle. He asks me if other people in our village also ride a bicycle.

"Not many. Most of them drive trucks."

He asks if they have very far to go and very much to carry.

"Some do, most don't."

"Then why they no ride bicycle? Bicycle is beautiful."

Snatches of conversation travel among us and we move

at a steady pace, clambering over hills and dropping into
ravines, fording streams sometimes up to our waists. The
tropical heat presses down on us as it does on all pink
people. The air is viscid, like breathing muslin. Around
every bend I peer as far ahead as I can, expecting to see our
porters. After several hours it occurs to me that we might
never see our boats, or any of our gear, ever again.

We reach Keressadji at two in the afternoon. The soft
white feet inside our boots are flayed. We are scratched,
covered in mud, drenched in sweat. Sori looks unscathed.
His skin is dry, his white shirt still white, fedora jaunty as
ever.

When the porters see us, they yell and wave happily. They
are sitting in the shade beside a pile of banana peels. They
have been waiting for us for two hours. Only three of them
are left. Two have already gone back to their separate
villages. All of them still have a full day's work to do.

Sori presents us before the chief of the village of Keressadji,
as he did before the chief of Bambaya. It is a protocol that
will be repeated in every village we pass through in the
Fouta Djallon. It always begins with an ancient, prescribed
litany between the chief and the traveler.

"Chief ass first how it iss where we come from."

"What do you say, Sori?"

"I say iss good where we come from."

"What if it is not good?"

"Chief already know if iss good or not good."

"Then?"

"Then chief ass of my family. My mother and my father.
My seesters and my brothers. All family."

Sori might say they are well but the chief will know better
and ask about his uncle who cut his leg with a mattock or
the little girl with the problem in her eyes.

If the traveler is a man of stature, he will in turn ask the
chief about his village, his clan. This can be risky. The chief

will say all is well. But in a remote village it is never so; something has always happened. The traveler must know what is wrong—who is sick, who has died—and inquire after it. Not to do so is to reveal his insincerity.

Sori has such stature. He knows all the chiefs and their villages. He knows what to ask and whom to ask after.

The chief will then ask how Sori himself is and Sori will say he is very well thank you, a reply he would make if he had been mauled by a leopard. The chief will ask about the journey to his village and Sori will say it was uneventful, mentioning only in passing that a bridge has been carried off or the path on a treacherous side-slope washed away.

Only when the chief asks of news will Sori explain what he is doing bringing four white men into the chief's village. The chief will listen, moving his eyes over each of us one at a time. Then the chief will begin to smile, realizing he is a host. Baskets of oranges will be carried into the hut. We will each take just one, trying to be polite, and the chief will thunder and the women will spill a half dozen into each of our laps. Water will be brought in calabashes and we will try to avoid drinking it by showing our satisfaction with our own water bottles.

Later we will be shown to our quarters, a large gazebo-like hut in the middle of the village that serves as the town hall. It has a tall straw roof supported by wooden poles. The village will gather to watch us unroll our sleeping bags and set up our tents on the clay floor. Some precocious child, for unknown reasons, will speak English.

Why do we sleep inside cocoons when we have a roof over our heads?

For the mosquitoes.

The child will translate for his village. The villagers will shake their heads at our fearfulness. Even those slack and jaundiced from malaria.

Mike will make buzzing sounds and close in on a small child and the child will hide behind her mother's leg and the crowd will laugh.

Where are we going?

Tembakounda.

They will look frightened. Tembakounda is not a good place for us to go.

Why?

There is war there. The child will make shooting sounds and gestures. Then he will ask us what is hidden in our great bags.

Boats.

The villagers will laugh again, slap their legs. No, this is not possible.

Boats! Boats for what?

The river?

What river?

A chicken will be killed in our honor. They will show it to us alive, kicking and crowing, then strangle it. An hour later the bird, beak and claws and muscle and viscera, will be returned to us in a hot pepper stew along with rice and cassava and more fruit.

After we have eaten and it is night, the chief will reappear, striding out of the darkness in his flowing caftan and pointed slippers. He will want to talk. This is our chance to repay his kindness. This is the duty of a traveler in remote lands—that which those who do not journey do not understand: Good travel is an exchange, food and shelter for much-sought-after discourse, succor for stories. The host receives more than he gives; the traveler receives more than he takes.

Once his village has gathered, the chief will ask us questions. There are no TVs in his village. Someday TVs will arrive but there are none now. We are entertainment and education. The chief will not ask us about our journey through his land. He knows we do not understand what we have seen. He knows we are foreigners up to something foolish. Besides, his people already know their own country.

Sori will translate both ways and the chief will ask us what our homes look like. How big or small? What is snow?

Do we drive airplanes? What food do we eat? What work do we do? What faith do we have? Anything that interests him or he believes should interest his village. The chief wants only the truth. He does not want to be patronized; he wants perspective. He wants to understand the world he cannot see.

The chief's wives are whispering in his ear.

"Sori, tell him we will answer any question."

"Chief say in Merica iss possible only for to hahve one wife?"

"That is true."

"Chief say iss bad. He want know how many children you have."

"None yet. Soon."

I point to myself and then Michael. The chief's wives place their dark eyes on us, appraising.

"Chief sprised. He ass how many children Merica man hahve."

"Usually two. Sometimes less, sometimes more."

"Chief say iss bad. He say white people no love children."

"Sori, tell the chief we do love children."

"Chief say you rich. You should—"

The chief interrupts Sori.

"He say if you no hahve many children, you love money more than children."

"Probably true," whispers Rick, nodding his head. John agrees.

"Bullshit," says Mike.

"Sori, ask the chief how many children he has."

"He say many children."

"Why?"

"He say he love children."

"Sori, ask the chief what his children do."

Someone has brought out more candles. We can see the chief better now. He is surrounded by his village, a hundred faces. He holds up both hands and begins speaking, flicking off his fingers.

"Chief say two boys study Koran to bless family. Three,

67

four boys stay home make farm business. Two, three boys go city make money."

"What about the girls?"

The chief grins broadly. He is surprised by our apparent ignorance.

"He say girls work."

"Tell the chief his children are his money."

Sori's eyes swing around and hit me.

"Tell him."

The chief says nothing. His clan stirs nervously, their eyes darting from their chief to me and swiftly back to their chief.

"Ask the chief what the boys in the city do with the money they make."

"Chief say boys send money to chief."

"Ask the chief what the boys who are farming do."

"He say boys sell rice for chief."

"Who farms the rice? Who works the fields?"

"Women. Girls."

"Sori, tell the chief that in America sons do not have to give money to their fathers."

"Chief say because father not love boy. If father love boy, boy give money. If boy no give money, boy bad."

"In America it is the other way around. The father gives money to his sons. And to his daughters."

"Chief say why? Daughters no need money."

"And the sons?"

"Chief say boy young. Boy strong. Father give boy life. Boy no give father life."

"Untrue. The son gives his father joy. Is joy not life?"

A smile gradually spreads across the chief's face.

"Sori, what does the chief do with his money?"

The chief laughs and shows his teeth and turns his great head looking around him and spreads his arms out above his clan like huge wings. Then he claps his hands once, loudly, and rises. The palaver is over.

"Tell the chief thank you for his hospitality and conversation."

Sori stands up and turns to us.

68

"Chief say he thank you too. He say he wish Allah to travel with us."

In the morning we have new porters. We will hike to the village of Foroconia, twenty miles deeper and higher into the mountains. The porters have already left, their leather feet padding silently through the jungle, our bags balanced on their heads like giant eggs, our boats inside waiting as patiently as baby crocodiles—legs and tails folded, skin soft, eyes gummy.

Sori and I take to the trail together. We have become companions. The path weaves up and down, cutting across the grain of the jungle. We have not seen the Niger. There are no footpaths along the Niger because there are no villages there. The river is unknown. Lost in the jungle as if it were a subterranean river. It is unknown because it is unnecessary. We are in a rain forest. Water is everywhere. We are wading or leaping streams all day long. And every afternoon it rains. Rain such as I have never seen anywhere on earth.

There is no warning. No random raindrops sent as messengers of the forthcoming sprinkle that itself is but a harbinger of the real thing. Thunder explodes and you jump and in the time it takes to lift your head it is pouring. Nay, deluging. As though the entire Atlantic Ocean were sucked up into the sky and blown up over Sierra Leone and released upon the mountains. The path metamorphoses into a deep sluice racing against your legs making you slip and flounder and clutch at plants. The forest turns into breakers of thrashing green. Even the air itself shape-shifts. Gasping for oxygen you instead breathe in warm liquid as in a dream where you have been transformed into an animal with gills.

Then the rain vanishes. Just like that. As if a huge rubber plug were suddenly rammed into a hole in the sky. The air, no longer hysterical, becomes itself again, moist but composed, and the water runs off down the trail.

When the rain comes, the villagers take refuge beneath the straw soffits of their mud huts and peer through the thick curtain of water. If they are out in the fields, they squat under ponchos of palm leaves. After it passes, everyone goes on about their business. The men resume lashing poles together for a new school; the women step back into the fields; little children run out and start splashing the blue puddles with their tiny hands and laughing.

I tread right behind Sori; Mike and Rick and John follow some ways behind.

Sori neither walks nor runs; he glides, like a panther. He moves without thinking. Without looking down, he skips over the thorncreepers strung across the path like barbwire, skirts the booby traps of fluted roots, hops the swift brown runnels. He passes ephemerally through webs of light and shadow and I follow directly in his footsteps, trying to remember the rhythm of motion.

The path divides itself over and over. At each parturition Sori veers left or right without hesitation. It is natural for him. He is primordial. His compass is inside.

Today Sori is telling me the story of his family, which is the story of this kingdom. When I am listening to him, when I am inside the story, I too can glide. The story transports me. My breathing regulates itself and my legs operate on their own. Only when the sound of his voice stops do I become conscious of my body, try to guide my feet, and stumble.

But then, when I begin to tell a story, the grace comes back and we again move in unison through the trees. It is as if motion itself were the story.

Sori is the youngest grandson of the last king of the feudal mountains of the Fouta Djallon. Sori's grandfather was the ruler of 272 villages. He had forty-six wives. Untold children. Sori's own father had thirty-seven wives. Sori has thirty-eight older brothers.

I ask him if he knows all their names.

"Ahmoudal al, Achmed, Bassi, Bellabaswa, Bin al Kamin, Bondi, Coocoorasa, Cessia . . ."

He names them all. One name for one stride. Thirty-eight strides.

I ask him if he has always lived here, in the mountains.

"No," he says. "When Sori young man, Sori want travel. Sori travel much. Live in much places. Nigeria. Monrovia. Côte d'Ivoire."

He was working in Ghana when a letter sent the year before came to him saying he must return to his village. His people were slowly starving. They needed him. He returned.

"What did you do?"

"I do what I can do. Everything."

He began selling grain, bartering illegal cat skins, guiding geologists. Buying and selling. Carrying cloth or clothing or knives or jewels on his bicycle on the paths through the jungle.

In every village we have passed through, he has given out money. It is the money we gave him to guide us. He always gives it to a woman.

"Men drink money."

"I thought Muslims did not drink."

He smiles over his shoulder. "We not all Muslims yet, Mahk."

After two hours of hiking Sori stops in a patch of sunlight. I look back down the trail. We have lost Mike and Rick and John. I think Sori has stopped to let them catch up, but that is not the reason.

"I pray now."

Sori steps off the trail, drops his pack, slips off his plastic sandals, kneels and places his fedora on the ground in front of him. Sitting back on his heels he begins to chant. He bows forward, touches his forehead to the ground, holds it there, and continues to murmur.

It is a rite. Sori prays five times a day. Doesn't matter where we are or what we're doing; he stops and prays.

I am not ready to stop. I have a good sweat going and feel

oiled and strong. We are deep in the mountains now and I am at home. But I unleash myself from my pack and sit down. At the next fork in the trail I wouldn't know which direction to go.

I lie back in the grass and begin to relax. The heat of the jungle enfolds me. My body is in the sun but my head is in the shade. I turn and stare at the soles of Sori's feet. They are like paws. The hide half an inch thick, rough and cracked, imbedded with thorns.

I close my eyes and let my mind wander. Listen to the forest. A monkey calling, birds, so many birds, unknown animals scurrying in the underbrush, and inside it all, his incantation. It is a sound that comes from deep within him. A hum. A psalm.

It grows distant. I don't hear it stop.

In the afternoon Sori and I are passing along a mountain-side scored with rivulets—water sliding out of the jungle, cutting across our path and disappearing back into the jungle. We haven't been talking, just moving together, when he asks me to name my brothers.

"Steven, Daniel, Christopher."

His eyes slip back.

"Seesters."

"Pamela and Wendy."

"Iss all?"

"That is all."

He is sorry for me. My blood is not as deep as his.

I tell him my mother was one of seven children and my wife has seven brothers and sisters. This lightens him. He asks me if I know all my aunts and uncles and cousins. I tell him I do. He asks me to name them. It is more than a hundred people. When I finish he grins over his shoulder.

"Then you child coming will be strong!"

At that moment, as if a grenade has gone off on the trail right in front of me, I see Sue.

She is standing at the window. The glass is cold on her forehead. There is no sound. Snow is swimming down through the arms of the cottonwoods to lie with itself in drifts across the yard. Our child is moving in her and she touches it, feels a foot slide across the globe.

She looks up and sees me, here, sweating, tramping through the jungle to the source of some river. There is a vague smile on her face.

We look at each other for a moment, me from Africa and her from Wyoming as if all the distance between us were but a pane of glass.

Then we both blink and return to where we are.

We must do this. We have learned how to do this. It has taken many years. It is the only way to live apart. The only way to live alone and not let longing tear you to pieces.

Sori and I have reached a saddle and begin descending a slope strewn with gigantic boulders. I have been behind him all morning. I jump up out of the trail and pass him, leaping boulder to boulder, flying down through the air. Massive trees with bark punctured by two-inch thorns crowd the boulder field. One slip and I would impale myself, or break an ankle, or a leg. But I won't slip.

At the bottom of the slope I stop, turn around, and look up. Sori is winding his way along the path between the boulders. Mike appears at the top and starts cautiously bounding down through the talus. I watch him leaping block to block, zigzagging down the steep slope. He stops once, teetering on the edge of a big drop, halloos and waves.

In Marrakesh we smoked hash and slurped green goulash from wooden bowls in the Medina and slept on rooftops awaking before dawn to the cry of the muezzin. We watched a little boy get his tooth pulled in the street, the dentist using pliers and a foot-pump drill. Kid didn't even flinch. We saw a Berber stab his camel with a sword. I almost got into a knife fight I would have lost.

We never showered or shaved or saw a mirror. We thought of ourselves as wild and gallant and followed our noses straight into trouble we escaped only through pure luck. We assumed we would come out of every scrape unscathed. It is a naive and groundless faith but it is what you believe when you are eighteen, and because you believe it, it often works.

From Marrakesh, Mike wanted to head for Timbuktu via the beach, along the Atlantic coast; I wanted to go due south through the mountains. We did rock-paper-scissors and I won and we hopped a bus bound into the Atlas.

The bus was a windowless cage on bald tires. The engine wheezed like an old man. The higher we inched into the mountains the slower the bus moved. When a donkey cart passed us, we couldn't take it anymore. We dropped our packs from the overhead rack and jumped off. The bus driver shrugged and the passengers stared. We thought we could walk faster than the bus. It turned out we couldn't, but because the bus stopped so frequently, hours later we could still see it creeping around the switchbacks high above us.

On our map it looked as if the road we were on went right past the highest peak in the Atlas Mountains, Jebel Toubkal, 13,665 feet. We figured we might as well climb it.

We slept in the dirt beside the road and set out up a steep valley early the next morning. We moved fast passing one hillside village after another. Late in the afternoon we abandoned the trail and cut up to a ridge. We were hoping to get a view, and we did. We were quite high but miles away from the peak.

"Mike. We went up the wrong valley. We have to backtrack."

"I guess."

He didn't look right.

"You okay?"

"Feeling a little strange."

"Let's get down before it is dark."

It was a beautiful evening. Not a cloud, the sky a Parrish blue. The lower the sun dropped, the richer the colors became. The Atlases are desert mountains and the soil and the stones and the rock arêtes all passed through ever deepening shades of sienna.

Near the base of the ridge we entered a vast boulder field. Massive, jumbled blocks all balancing at the angle of repose. I began springing boulder to boulder, flying through the cool evening air.

"This is just like Vedauwoo!" I called back.

Vedauwoo was the rock climbing area outside Laramie. The word means "earth born" in Arapahoe. After Coach taught us how to climb, Mike and I went to Vedauwoo all the time. At the end of a day, having sufficiently bloodied ourselves trying to scale some little rock wall, we would play a game we'd dubbed "Jesus jumping." The name came from some fuzzy combination of our theories on fear and death and religion.

"Jesus jumping" was simply leaping from one boulder down to another. The greater the drop and the greater the distance, the more hallowed the jump. We had names for different categories of jumps. Little jumps, say five or six feet across and a few feet down, were "priest jumps." Add a few feet to the distance and the drop and you had a "bishop jump." Increase both again and it was a "cardinal jump." Beyond that it got hairy. There was the "pope jump" and the "Jesus jump." The Jesus jump was a leap of such enormous faith, a leap of such irreversible danger, that it scared you to think that you would even think about it.

There were three parts to any jump: the takeoff, the flight, and the landing. You always took off from one foot and then brought your feet together in the midair. In flight you had to stay vertical, tense but somehow also loose, anticipating the landing. Because the boulders were piled willy-nilly down a steep slope, the touchdown had to be executed perfectly. If you landed off balance and had to take a lunging step in any direction, you'd be forced to jump again, or fall. Either way you'd break a leg, or worse. To land right it helped to think about how a cat lands, legs apart, knees flexed, the whole body absorbing the shock.

After a couple seasons of this game Mike and I were making priest jumps and bishop jumps all the time. Once in a while, when we were feeling brave, we'd pull off a cardinal jump. Pope jumps were extremely rare. You had to be in a special mood and even then after you'd done it and lived through it you always thought it was a pretty dumb thing to do. Mike never tried a pope jump. Neither of us ever tried what we considered a Jesus jump. We thought ourselves quite mature for this.

Bounding down through the boulders in the High Atlas Mountains of Morocco I was feeling vibrantly alive, invincible. For the first time in my life I was utterly free. Emancipated.

I wasn't even noticing the little jumps. I kept steering my path through the blocks to take advantage of the biggest drops. Several times I stopped and looked back at Mike. He seemed to be doing fine but I was enjoying myself too much to really notice. I kept making bigger and bigger jumps, flying through the cool azure air as if coming off a trampoline. Before I knew it, I'd made a jump I didn't want to. I leapt out into space and then I was there for too long. It didn't feel right. I was dropping too slowly and it seemed to take forever to land and then the soles of my boots struck the rock and the jolt rammed straight up through my spine and I screamed from the pain. I stayed in a crouch for almost a minute, trying to assess the damage, then straightened up.

"*Mark!*"

Mike was above me looking down.

"It's kind of a drop."

"It's a fucking *Jesus jump!*"

"No it's not. It's just a pope."

Mike was kneeling, peering down at me. His face didn't look right at all now. It was puffy. His skin was pallid, almost green.

"Mike, you don't look good."

"I'm all right." He stood back up.

Suddenly I knew he wouldn't make it. I saw it all—saw

him falling instead of jumping, dropping through the African sky like a limp child.

He was stepping back to get a run at it.

"*Mike!*"

He moved back to the edge so I could see him. "What?"

"Don't do it."

"Why?"

"Just don't do it, okay."

"It's just another jump, Buck."

"Mike. Don't."

We looked into each other's eyes until we both felt embarrassed.

"Hey. Okay. No sweat. If it makes you happy."

He walked along the edge of the boulder and found a different way down. I waited for him. When he came up to me, he put his arm around my shoulder and hung there.

Mike had pulmonary edema, severe altitude sickness. The body fails to adjust to the elevation and the lungs begin to malfunction, slowly filling with fluid. The victim can die in a matter of hours if he doesn't retreat to a lower altitude.

But we didn't know this at the time. Hell, we'd grown up in the mountains. We both thought he was just a little sick. Bad food maybe. We didn't find out how dangerously susceptible Mike was to altitude sickness until three years later.

We were on Denali, Mount McKinley, in Alaska. We were at 14,400 feet. I awoke in the middle of the night. Mike was saying something. I switched on my headlamp and found him sitting up in his sleeping bag.

"You want to hear the ocean, Buck?"

I thought he was dreaming. We'd spent so much time in a tent together, we both had wild tales of what the other had said in his dreams.

"Go back to sleep, Mike."

"I can't breathe."

Then I noticed he was in an awkward position. He was

gray. His hands and face were bloated. He had torn off his undershirt.

I leaned over and put my ear against his chest. I could hear sloshing, gurgling. His lungs were full of liquid. He was drowning.

The chief of Foroconia doesn't look like the other village chiefs. He's wearing pants, a blue shirt, red sneakers. There is a man standing behind him wearing a green uniform with stripes on the epaulets. Sori and the chief have been talking for a long time but the chief has not smiled. Something is wrong.

Eventually Sori turns to us.

"Chief say no possible. He say too much killing."

Tembakounda is less than a day's walk away, but the chief cannot allow us to go there. To reach Tembakounda we must cross the border and pass briefly through Sierra Leone. There is a war in Sierra Leone. It has been going on for years. It is as heinous and senseless as all war. The soldiers have weapons so they don't die so much. The defenseless die. Children, women, boys. Shot or macheted or blown to pieces.

Rick and John don't speak. Mike shakes his head. He asks Sori if the chief wants money. He is hoping it's just a matter of extortion. People are easily bribed. That is the way things get done in most countries. It is the fast way to get your way.

Sori says no, it is not about money. We have entered the chief's domain. He is responsible for us.

I ask Sori to tell the chief that we are adults and that we will be responsible for ourselves. Sori does so reluctantly. The chief frowns. It was the wrong thing to say. Everything that happens in the chief's domain is the chief's responsibility. Sori stops listening to us. He asks us to leave so he can talk to the chief alone.

We erect our tents in the tall hut in the middle of the village. Rick relaxes quietly; Mike starts to read; I take a few pictures. John transforms a page of his journal into a swan and gives it to the village children. Sori reappears after an hour.

"Chief say okay. Chief hahve men go with us."

At dawn we are given a six-man escort. Only two of them look like soldiers; one is a schoolteacher. Several of them have rifles. I inspect their weapons. One is missing the firing pin; one is plugged with rust. Mike and I place our Rugers and two clips at the top of our packs. We say nothing to Rick or John.

We have no porters. The boats will stay here. There is no watercourse above us big enough to boat. We will walk up to the source of the Niger, then come back down and search for the river.

We leave the village sandwiched between our escort. Three men in front of us, three men in back of us, Sori out ahead as scout. The trail becomes steep immediately, switch-backing up a floral ravine. After two miles we gain a plateau. A millennium of foliage has corrugated the surface. We tramp through ditches running with water, the jungle hanging above us.

I think we are tending east and ask Mike.

"That's what I was thinking. Doesn't feel right, does it?"

At a rest break we ask Sori.

"Seems like we should be heading west."

Sori cocks his head at us. We are correct. But he says we can't go straight to the source. We would be stopped by cliffs. He grins and adjusts his fedora and tells us that sometimes you have to go all the way around something to get to it.

The path moves up high contouring along the flanks of a mountain before dropping into a cuplike valley planted with rice. There are scarecrows stuck out in the shimmering, stem-pricked water. On a trail circling the field we discover a naked child hiding beneath a plant. He has a string in his hand. He looks up at us but does not speak.

Sori says when the birds come to steal the rice, the boy will jerk the string and the scarecrows will rock back and forth and the birds will be scared away. Rick and John and Mike and I nod. But after we have passed the child, Mike and I go around the soldiers and catch up to Sori.

"That's not true."

He shakes his head. "Sori say only true things. That child watching."

"For birds."

"Yes."

"But not birds with wings."

"No."

"Birds with guns perhaps."

"Perhaps."

Africans sometimes speak in allegories. But then often-times they don't. The hard part is knowing when they are and when they aren't.

Across the valley we rise into a forest on the back side of the mountain. We have passed into Sierra Leone now. It is obvious. The soldiers have stopped talking. Their eyes dart side to side and they have swung their rifles into their hands.

We are no longer in jungle. The vines and underbrush are gone and the trees are slim and well spaced. More light comes through. The air is lighter, brighter. We are rising toward the ridge.

Our trail intersects another trail on the ridgeline. We turn right and begin moving through open woods along the crest. Suddenly we have views. Between the trees on either side a solid mass of green falls away. We are on the divide, the fulcrum. All the water that falls to our left has a short swift trip down to the Atlantic. The beach is only two hundred miles to the west. All the water that falls to our right has a great pilgrimage—a three-thousand-mile odyssey across West Africa.

When we reach a lookout facing north, Sori points down at a small, deep saddle.

"*Tembakounda*," he whispers.

The four of us stand together and stare down at the place. It looks exactly like a dozen other saddles we have passed through.

"That's it?" asks John. "Right there?"

"Yes," says Sori.

We skid down the slippery path, passing the soldiers,

laughing, wanting to shout but afraid to. The path runs through the forest to a small dry clearing in the middle of the saddle. We stop and wait for Sori and our escort to catch up.

"Where's the water, Sori?"

Sori points east.

"Where?"

His face is wooden, expressionless.

"In the trees?"

"Yes."

The soldiers have squatted in the sunlight with their rifles between their knees. They are restless. Their eyes search the shadows.

"Okay. We go now."

"No, Sori. Where is the spring?"

Sori points down into the trees again.

"Will you show us?"

He shakes his head. He is clearly frightened.

I ask him what the problem is. He says the spring is sacred. He says we are white people and not from here and not staying here so we can do what we want but he can't go with us. If he were to go to the spring, it would put a curse on his entire family.

"You go!" Sori drops onto his haunches and looks away.

The four of us slip off our packs and walk into the woods. We spread out like hunters. The forest is thick enough that soon we can't see each other. We are on a gentle slope that drops quickly down through the trees. After a few minutes I stop. I hear something. Someone is shouting.

I move toward the voice through the forest. It seems to be coming up out of the ground. I am going fast, kicking up the leaves, when I almost fall into a hole hidden in the forest floor. I get down on my stomach and peer over the edge.

"Here it is!"

Mike is down inside the hole. It's like a cave. A dense net of roots hangs over him—thin black limbs as if thousands of people were buried here. I hold on to the rigid arms and lower myself into the pit.

Mike is up against the back wall beneath an overhang of
soil. Rivulets are seeping out of the wall into a dark pool at
his feet. He squats and cups up a handful of water.

"Take a drink! It's sweet."

I sink down on my hands and knees, put my lips to the
surface of the pool like an animal, and drink. Then we both
shove our hands into the source of the Niger and lift them
out like bowls and hold them over our heads and ribbons of
quicksilver spill through our fingers into our faces and down
our necks.

Mike stands up, holds on to a crooked limb, and throws
his head back.

"Riiiiickkk. Jooooohhnn."

After a few minutes they appear above us on the edge of
the hole.

"Is this it?"

They back down into the grotto, holding on to the roots.
They too drink from the source. For a few minutes we stand
together around the tiny pool in the womb of the earth and
don't speak. The water is like a mirror. We can see our own
reflections. We can see each other's reflections.

We shake hands and snap a team photo and then John
says, "Well, boys, time to start boating."

We help each other up out of the cave, pulling on the
roots. I am the last one out. Mike and Rick and John head
up through the trees. I hold back for one last look.

I stare down at the pool. It is absolutely still, as if it were
a solid. But then at one end where the cave opens up there
is a translucent thread of water spinning out of the cavity
and disappearing down into the woods. It makes me smile.

The pool only appears motionless. It stays the same size
and shape and yet it is never the same pool. It is water passing through itself. The pool is only an illusion.

When we get back to the saddle, the soldiers are on their
feet. Sori says we must go now, quickly.

"Iss no place for to stay."

He says we are on the border trail. There could be a patrol somewhere. Armed men. Our escort leads the way, practically running.

In three hours we are back in Guinea. I catch one of the soldiers sighing, another wiping the sweat off his upper lip. Sori pulls in beside me and locks an arm around mine and we walk together, letting everyone else bound ahead.

"Tembakounda iss well?"

He asks it of me as if he were a chief inquiring after my father or my mother or my family.

"Yes. Sori, thank you very much."

He nods. He has done what he said he could do. We walk for a ways arm in arm.

But something is troubling me. In fact, it has been bothering me since we first began our hike into the mountains. I haven't said anything. I've kept it to myself because I didn't want to destroy the myth.

"Sori. Why is that place Tembakounda?"

He doesn't answer.

"I mean why that particular place? Why not some other place? Water is everywhere." I point in different directions.

"We must have passed scores of springs."

Sori shakes his head. "Tembakounda. Tembakounda."

He doesn't want to talk about my doubts. It is not for him to question such things. When I press him, he unlinks his arm and starts moving off down the trail. I am left alone in the rain forest.

When Mike and I first dreamed up this trip, we wanted to start at the source. Starting at the source seemed poetic.

Beginning at the beginning. That single limpid drip that grows into a brook that matures into a stream that one day becomes a river. But hiking up here we have crossed hundreds of such brooklets. All of them purling quietly downhill, becoming blue or black or green streams that will converge in a thousand confluences before becoming one great river.

Tembakounda could not be the source of the Niger. The

source of the Niger is a fiction. A river becomes a river not from one source but from hundreds, thousands. Rivers are born in watersheds. To begin at the beginning is impossible.

Night falls before we make it back down to Foroconia. We have to bivouac in a village called Farakoro. The villagers are suspicious. They live on the edge of war. They peer mute and white-eyed from behind their wood doors and don't speak to us.

We leave before light and trek all the way back to Keressadji, doing two days in one because it is downhill. The boats come down with us. They needn't have even gone up.

So high in the watershed the Niger is still a labyrinth beneath the jungle, all the streams too small even for a kayak.

In Keressadji we are welcomed back like men given up for dead. We have returned alive from where no one should go. They are joyous for us, for our luck. They know it is all you have and that you can lose it easily and quickly.

But we are spent. We move slowly setting up our tents inside the hut. It is night by the time we finish. We drop onto the dirt floor and use our headlamps to examine each other's feet. Our soles are bloody, bandaged with swaths of duct tape.

A platter of spiced rice and meat appears and we think we are too tired to eat until we start eating.

Then the drums.

We were going to sleep. Lie down flat on our backs and close our eyes and smile at how good it feels to lie flat after walking all day for days. It didn't rain in the afternoon so it is going to rain tonight. We were going to lie back and fall instantly into an ocean of sleep and not dream until we heard the rain and then still not carry the burden of our dreams but simply listen to the water inside our sleep.

But then the drums.

The women of the village crowd into the hut and stand above our tents and begin teasing us.

What are you men doing! You are men, yes?

It is not the time to sleep; it is the time to rejoice!

You have been to *Tembakounda* and returned safely. You must get up! Tomorrow you will leave. You will say you will return but you never will. Tomorrow you will begin another journey and be gone forever so tonight you must dance!

They haul us out of the hut. There is a great crowd. The bonfire is already springing into the black sky. Again there are three drums and three drummers. One of the drummers is the same man who drummed in Bambaya our first night in the jungle. I wonder how he has come here. How he heard the news that the four white men made it up to Tembakounda and back.

This time the drummers do not search for the right sound. Tonight the drums need not talk. Tonight the drums shall wail. They pull them from the fire and slam them between their legs and the sound is like thunder, as if a tempest were bursting over the village.

We stand in the circle with the women letting the sound roll into us. It is not music. You hear music. Music goes into your ears. Drums are discharges. They hit you in the stomach and chest and make your legs quiver.

The women begin singing. They are clapping their hands and singing with their heads thrown back, their necks thick, their warm tongues moving in their open mouths.

Women come toward us, across the circle through the sound as if they are swimming through liquid. Each of us is taken by the hand into the circle and then Mike and John and Rick and Sori and I are dancing and all the women of the village are pouring in letting themselves go leaping and laughing and clapping their hands.

The woman who chose me has slid one leg between my thighs and is undulating in waves. She is against me thrusting and rocking, moving me with her hips, her shoulders back her breasts pushed upward her fingers twitching as if the shock of the drums were a current going through us.

Another woman comes against my side and the two together enclose me between their hips and legs slowly turning until they face away and the orbs of their buttocks are grinding against me holding me in the flood of their flesh.

Sometime late in the night it begins to rain and we are still dancing, we have never stopped dancing, and it rains for hours. Then the rain stops and the moon comes out and we are still dancing, the tongues of the women trilling and their bodies dripping in the moonlight, their wet breasts swinging, their electric hips throbbing, their feet—the great heavy weapons of their life—cracking the ground in unison.

THE RIVER

We are searching for the river in the jungle. We have been searching for two days. You wouldn't think something so big and obvious would be so difficult to find.

In the middle of the afternoon Sori stops at the intersection of two trails. We are surrounded by towering trees roped together with lianas. Sori speaks to the porters. They drop our bags and take a seat in the grass. Sori looks at us and points down the trail to our left.

"Gentlemahns, the Niger."

It's a half-hour walk downhill, the path a trough through blue shadows. The jungle is so dense we don't see the river until we are standing on its bank.

There is a bridge flung over the seething water. A tight-rope of green poles lashed together with vines. It hangs from the crotch of one tree to the crotch of another on the opposite bank. One by one we climb up through the tree and tiptoe out along the bouncy poles. Sori waits on the bank.

The river is a brown torrent. It appears out of a cave of jungle, shoots beneath us, rushes headlong through the trees for a short distance, bends, and disappears.

It is the first time we have seen the river since Faranah. John is shaking his head.

"Forget it, guys. Strainers everywhere."

Rick nods vigorously.

"What'd you say? Something about colanders?" Mike is

climbing off the bridge, hanging like a monkey by one arm and one leg to get a closer look at the path of the water.

"Strainers are no bullshit, Mike."

"I know, John."

Strainers are things hidden in a river that can catch you. Limbs or roots or vines concealed just beneath the opaque surface that can grab your boat and flip it over. Sometimes you can swim out but sometimes the force of the current traps you upside down and you drown.

"Half the damn jungle's been washed into the river." John is earnest. "Strainers could split our boats wide open!"

Mike isn't listening. He's hanging off the bridge, peering down the channel.

"Just look at the current!" John points at the brown water. It is boiling from its own power. The trees on the banks are deeply submerged.

I am searching for the telltale signs of strainers. Dimples, bobbing limbs, elbows of wood poking up through the surface. Of course the dangerous ones are those you don't see until they've already got you.

"Damn it!" John is incredulous. "One of us could get impaled on a broken branch."

"Could," says Mike.

John doesn't take another look. He carefully retreats off the bridge and heads back up the trail. Rick and Sori go with him.

Mike and I study the tunnel the river has gouged through the jungle.

Mike is sanguine, as always. "Maybe it'll go."

"Maybe it won't."

"Guess we'll just have to see."

He swings himself back up onto the bridge, pulls his shirt over his head, and hangs it on a branch. He does it casually, as if he were undressing in a locker room, putting his shirt in the locker. Gracefully balancing on one foot and then the other, he takes off his boots and socks.

"You don't have to do this."

"It's not moving that fast, Mark."

"It's moving fast. It's deceptive. We can just use a stick. Watch."

I break off an overhanging limb and drop it into the river. The current catches it and spins it in circles, rushing it downstream. It vanishes around the bend in seconds.

Mike is stripping off his pants. "Doesn't tell us much, does it?"

"If it carries you away, I won't be able to help you."

"Yes you will."

"How?"

"You'll think of something."

"It's stronger than it looks."

"Yup."

He's naked now. He lowers himself into the river hanging on to the bridge. The water pulls on his body, stretching him out.

"Tell you what"—he's grinning madly—"I'll pretend my body's a boat."

"Remember what Sori said?"

Mike doesn't answer. He's hanging in the water looking downstream, planning his course.

Sori told us not to get into the water because there are tiny spiderfish that swim up your dick and then spread their hooked spines. Sori also told us there were whirlpools in the river, black vortexes that swallowed everything—animals, humans, even crocodiles. Swallowed them and they vanished forever.

Mike is twirling by one arm.

"How deep do you think it is?"

"Deep. Real deep."

"Good." Mike grins up at me again, then lets go.

Immediately he is stroking powerfully upstream but the river spins him around as easily as it did the stick and he is trying to swim toward the bank but sliding away and then he is spun hard and sent headfirst downstream and he reaches up barely catching a vine and the vine sinks but doesn't snap and he's flipped over like a fish pulled up out of the water.

He holds himself there with one arm. I can see the muscles in his chest, in his arm. The rest of his body is extended in the black water, jerking from the current.

He winks at me to reassure me, then lets go.

The river turns him again and he starts to go out of sight and I leap off the bridge and run along the river falling and stumbling, catching glimpses of him. I move out on a trunk hung over the water just in time to see him carried into a massive wall of jungle grown right over the river.

I back off the trunk and crash along the river looking for him through the trees and come out near the impenetrable wall of foliage. The river is wider and slower here, disappearing beneath the barricade as if dropping into a hole. I am standing on a limb searching. Mike is nowhere to be seen.

Suddenly I jump from a horrible growl. Something has snatched my ankle and is dragging me off the limb into the river.

"Jesus, Michael!"

"Aye, gotta watch out for dem crocs."

He throws himself up onto the branch in one motion, as if he were getting out of a swimming pool.

"I saw you disappear at the wall."

"Popped up inside like a cork, matey. She's a spiky cage in dere. A regular torture chamber." He's using his ridiculous pirate accent, rolling the rs, talking out the side of his mouth.

There are several deep scratches on his body. The blood is running in streaks down his legs.

"Souvenirs, I see."

"Aye, matey."

"So will it go?"

"I'm afraid she's jest a wee bit tight for d'ships."

We decided it was time for the beach. The next day we caught another bus and switchbacked out of the Atlas Mountains down to the Atlantic. When we saw the emerald-blue ocean, we dropped our packs and rushed into the water with our clothes on.

We pitched our tent in the thornbushes on shore and decided to stay forever.

Every morning we walked into the ocean naked. We had been told there were sharks but we paid no attention. Before our brains were even awake, our bodies were surfing. The waves were enormous. Dangerous. They attacked us. Rammed us into the sand and knocked the wind out of us. Rolled us into shore trying to break off our arms and legs. Dragged us across the sand rasping our sunburned bodies. We loved it.

In the middle of the day we hid from the sun in our hooch in the thornbushes and talked about girls and gazed at the crashing blue water.

In the evening, when the tide went out, we dug clams and tore up mussels and boiled them over driftwood for dinner. We listened to the pounding surf and talked about how far away we were. For breakfast we stole oranges from an orchard along the road, loading them into our shirts. Once every few days we walked to an Arab village down the coast and bought several round loaves of bread from black-robed women.

We couldn't imagine a better life. Living outdoors, living off the land. We were kings. Vagabond kings.

One night when we were lying in the sand around the campfire, Mike sprang to his feet.

"I got an idea. Let's swim out to the point."

"Right now? In the dark?"

"Why not?"

"The moon won't be up for at least an hour."

"That's right!"

Down on the beach noise surrounded us. The explosions of the surf were tremendous. They were so much louder when you couldn't see them. All we could make out were phosphorescent lines shimmering, then vanishing.

We kicked off our hiking boots and stripped off our

clothes and walked into the invisible water. It was mercurial, molten and cold. We shivered, gasped involuntarily. When it rose to our thighs, we shouted and dove in.

The cold made us swim hard, the mass of black weight chopping into us. Farther out, walls broke over our shoulders and shoved us under. In the pandemonium, we lost each other.

I kept swimming, trying to duck the waves, but I couldn't see them coming. Sometimes I could feel one approaching and managed to dive under at the right moment; sometimes I got hit. Eventually I swam through. Beyond the breakers each swell raised me into the abyss of night, held me there for a second, then gently let me down as the force moved on.

I stopped swimming and let my legs swing down. I could see absolutely nothing. It was amazing. The air itself seemed to have turned to ink.

I opened my mouth to shout for Mike but instead a screech came out. Suddenly I was kicking and writhing and screaming. Something had bitten my leg.

I knew it was circling for another attack and I couldn't tell if I still had a foot or if it was just jagged bone dangling bleeding into the water and I was slamming my thighs up and down and punching into the nothingness with my fists and then I heard a splash behind me and spun around and couldn't see a fucking thing.

"You thought I was a shark!"

"*Goddamn* you, Michael!"

He was gurgling with mirth, choking on the salt water.

"Where are you?"

"Right here."

I stirred myself toward the voice, pulling my arms in circles and kicking my legs. My foot brushed against something.

"Mike, that you?"

"That's me."

I could just make out something in front of me.

"It's wild, huh?"

I calmed myself down. I knew how to do this. I leaned my head back and stared up into the blackness. It was so dark it didn't matter if my eyes were open or closed. I listened to the water at my ears. It made soft clucking noises.

"You know what it's like, Mike? Remember hiding in the closet with somebody when you were a kid. How it was so dark you had to reach out and touch them to make sure they were there."

I waited for a response.

"Mike?"

"What?"

His voice was far away. In the pitch dark, we had drifted apart.

"Over here."

I heard splashing.

"Where are you?"

"Right here."

I heard more splashing.

"We should maybe try to stay close to each other."

"Fine by me."

We treaded water beside each other for a few minutes.

"Mike, what are you thinking about?"

"What it would be like to be lost at sea."

"C'mon."

"No, I am."

So I thought about it too. About those people who fall overboard sailing around the world or folks who are just on a short voyage when their ship is caught in a storm and founders and they're left bobbing in the ocean.

"How about you?"

"Oh, I'm thinking about sharks."

I hadn't been, really, but then maybe I was. On shore in the bright light of day I didn't think about sharks at all. I could hardly imagine them. But now in the stygian darkness I could see them plainly. Their blunt snouts and beady eyes, their massive, powerful bodies, their teeth like row after row of razors. It made me think about all the scrapes I had on my body. I wondered if any of them was leaking blood.

"Ready to swim for the point, Mike?"

"Sure."

"We should swim left."

"Left?"

"My left."

"No. Your right, my left." He was goofing around. Doing his who's-on-first routine.

"No really. We should swim left, don't you think?"

"Which way are you facing?"

"I don't know. I think I hear the surf to my left."

"I don't think you do."

"Which direction is it then?"

"How should I know?" he laughed.

"Mike. Really. Which direction do you think the shore is?"

I was expecting him to say something smart-aleck again.

"Mike?"

"Shhhhhhh. I'm trying to listen."

I tried to listen too. I slowly rotated myself in a circle. I didn't want to say anything. I wanted just to wait and hear the safe voice of the shore calling us like a mother calling her sons.

"Well?"

"I don't know."

We had drifted apart again. We moved toward each other.

"So." Mike's voice was different now. "Can you see any stars?"

I looked up. The blackness was so complete it was uncanny. It was as if we were underground.

"There must be a haze or something."

I knew what he was thinking. Mike was an Eagle Scout. All we had to do was find a constellation we could recognize; then we could reconnoiter. Find the Big Dipper, go straight up off the top of the lip, find the Little Dipper, find the North Star at the end of the handle, rotate to the right a quarter turn, swim east to shore. Nothing to it.

"You're right, there must be fog. I can't see a thing."

The fear was beginning, insinuating itself slowly, like a needle into the flesh of my belly. I tried to ignore it.

"It's funny."

"What?"

"It's just funny. I mean we can't tell any direction from any other direction. It's never happened to me before."

"It's not so funny, Mike."

"C'mon, Buck. What's the big deal? We can tread water all night if we have to."

I loosened up a little. Mike was right. We were strong. We could tread water for hours if we had to. I tried to go back to the way I was feeling before and enjoy being out here but something wouldn't let me.

"Mike."

"Yeah."

"We can't really tread water all night."

"Sure we can."

"I mean we can, but it won't matter."

"Why?"

"Because we're not just staying in one place. We can't feel it but the current is moving us. There's nothing we can do about it. By the time the sun comes up we could be out in the middle of the ocean."

I waited for him to refute me. I wanted him to refute me. He didn't answer.

We were keeping close to each other now, both smoothly treading water, once in a while intentionally brushing against each other. For a long time we didn't speak.

"Mike. We went too far this time."

"Maybe. Maybe just a little."

We kept treading.

"We should send a postcard tomorrow." His voice was soft and quiet.

"Yeah, we should."

Mike and I sent postcards instead of letters. With post-cards we didn't have to write so much. You could never explain to everybody back home what was really happening to you anyway. Some of it was what you saw and where you went but most of it was what was going on inside you. Every few weeks we sent one postcard from the both of us, alternating families. The family that got it was expected to pass it on after they read it.

"We could tell them about how we were saved by mermaids."

"Exactly."

"Mermaids used to save shipwrecked sailors all the time."

I put my head back. My eyes were open to the blackness. I treaded water. I tried to stay cool but I knew I was only pretending. It made me wonder if that was all staying cool really was.

Even though I didn't want it to, my mind kept returning to those people lost overboard. How they wouldn't have life jackets and so they would try to float but the waves would be too rough and they would have to tread water just like us. But then most of them wouldn't have much practice and wouldn't know how to conserve energy so they'd get tired fast. Then, too soon, they would start to think about what was going to happen to them.

Mike and I treaded for a long time without talking. I couldn't tell how long. I couldn't tell time anymore. Minutes, or maybe they were hours, kept expanding like balloons, then popping.

"Mark." Mike touched me with his foot. "I'm sorry."

I opened my eyes. "Yeah, we fucked up."

Just for a moment, the water and the air felt like the same substance. As if all I had to do was let myself sink and I would begin to breathe water as naturally as I breathed air.

"Hey listen." I touched Mike with my foot. "The sun'll come up and we'll see the shore and just swim for it, right."

"Sounds good."

Suddenly I thought I saw stars. My eyes were open and I was staring straight up into blackness and I thought I saw stars! But I wasn't sure. I didn't say anything. I could be wrong. I couldn't see them if I looked straight at them but if I looked kind of from the side I could see pricks of light in the black void.

"Mark?"

I was trying not to look right at them. I was desperate. I didn't want them to vanish. I was staring so hard my eyes were watering. I started trying to fill in the blank spaces between the stars. I was whispering inside myself over and over *God let that be the Big Dipper God let that be the Big Dipper.* But I didn't say anything. I still could be mistaken. Maybe it was all in my head. Maybe I was hallucinating. I'd read somewhere that sometimes that happened right before you died.

"Did you ever see those pictures of astronauts floating around in outer space?" Mike's voice was very calm. "The ones where the spaceship is far away and they're just out there with that long white string attached to them."

"Yeah, Mike, but—" I wanted to tell him to look up but I couldn't. I had to be certain.

Then two more stars sprang out. I was so ecstatic my rhythm got off and I wasn't treading water efficiently anymore and I started sinking, spitting water, laughing from the joy of hope.

"Well, Mark, it's like that string just broke."

For three days we move along paths that roughly parallel the river, cutting in wherever we can, searching for a place to start boating. Rick and John wait with the porters while Mike and I do the recon. We slip through the jungle until we find the river, then Mike jumps in.

Dougelema is the first village actually on the Niger. The four of us walk past the round mud huts to the wreck of a bridge spanning the turbid waters. It is the end of the monsoon season and the river is sweeping over the countryside, dragging in trees and bushes. The bridge is on stilts. A backbone of poles and planks held together with rope and spikes.

When we arrive, there are boys on the bridge. They are lined up on a board jutting out above the river. They are naked and taut and glistening, flinging themselves into the warm brown water. They are not afraid of the river. To them it's just water. They can barely swim but they don't think about it. They do not know what could lie under the surface. It doesn't occur to them. They are laughing gleefully, leaping before they look, jumping for the sheer joy of jumping.

We walk out onto the bridge and gaze downstream. It is a waterway of chocolate, running clean and flat for some distance before bending right and disappearing. The Niger seems to have finally cut a clear path.

"This is the place!" Mike chortles.

"But we can't see where it goes," says John. "We don't know what's around the bend."

"That's right," says Mike.

We assemble our boats surrounded by the village. They are spellbound. To them it is sorcery. Only wizards can draw sixteen-foot boats out of three-foot bags. But these are no ordinary boats. They were designed to be carried someplace remote and assembled. Doug Simpson, a taciturn Canadian from British Columbia, is the wizard.

The lifework of Doug Simpson was determined at the age of ten when he first paddled a kayak. He didn't know it then, but you never do. "It was the suppleness of a skin boat, how it glided through the water, that did it. The Eskimo kayak was and still is the quintessential one-man vessel."

Living as a squatter in an abandoned building on an island in Vancouver Bay, Simpson spent two decades fusing a prehistoric paradigm with twentieth-century technology. He replaced the sealskin shell with rubberized nylon, the spruce ribs and chines with aluminum tubing, the baleen joints with plastic. In the end his passion produced the finest collapsible kayak on earth. He named it the Feathercraft.

We midwife in teams, Mike and I, Rick and John. Sori watches quietly, standing in the circle of villagers.

It is like building a giant model airplane, or putting together the skeleton of some primeval amphibian. We lay out all the pieces and arrange them in order. The frame is assembled in two sections, the prow and the stern. Fit tube into tube, slot in the keel, snap the ribs into the vertebrae, stretch on the skin. Nest the combing into the cockpit, slot the rudder into the stern, hook up the rudder cables to the foot pedals. Everything logical and step-by-step, as if Simpson fully expected that one day his boat would be taken to Africa and assembled in the jungle at the head-waters of the Niger.

We work all afternoon, enjoying ourselves, psyching up for the river. Sori's eyes follow our every movement but he does not speak. His face is flat. He squats and hugs his knees. We don't need him any longer and it shows all over his body.

By dusk the boats are assembled. They lie in the dirt around us, as aboriginal as crocodiles. We will begin our journey down the Niger in the morning. John produces a Frisbee and delights the children.

Sori has had a woman prepare dinner. Our last supper. Sliced plantains in scalding orange sauce and bowls of pebbly millet. Later we are served chicken stew studded with lumps of squash. We banter among ourselves about what the river will be like. We are all eagerness and expectation but Sori is pensive and silent. Mike suggests that it's time we pay him. He's hoping it will cheer Sori up.

We give him what we agreed upon and throw in a little extra.

Sori asks for more.

Rick is insulted. He doesn't like to think of people living in the African bush as entrepreneurial. He likes to think of them as stoic and noble, happy with the way things are. To Rick, Sori's request is a sign that the scourge of capitalism has penetrated to the most remote places on earth.

We pay Sori more money. He is grateful. He asks if we're sure we don't want the cat skins. He'll give us a good price.

"No thank you, Sori," says John.

They are illegal cat skins, poorly cured hides of endangered species. But Sori doesn't assent to such abstract definitions. His family is endangered. He is feeding it any way he can.

He pulls me aside and asks if I am sure I don't want the gun barrel. He tells me again how he found it on his first trek to Tembakounda. I have told him before I am not interested but he still has hope. It's a heavy eight-inch length of gun barrel hirsute with rust. Could be a hundred years old, could be ten. The jungle eats everything. He wants two hundred dollars for it. Someone must have told him it was worth money. He had it in his gym bag the day we picked him up and has carried it the whole way hoping one of us would reconsider.

"I'm sorry, Sori."

"Yes." Sori smiles. He is disappointed. "You come here to see only."

"Yes."

"For little time. Short time. No for to stay."

I look at him.

"Better in Merica."

"America is our home."

"You come back?"

"Maybe."

"I no think you come back."

"Sori, I don't know."

"You friends in Merica come here?"

"I will tell them."

"You friends no come. I know."

What can I say?

"I be here."

"I know, Sori."

"You remember me. You remember Sori Keita."

"I will."

"You remember Sori Keita to you family."

"I will."

"Sori Keita here."

I will wish, for the rest of my life, that I had bought that corroded gun barrel.

The woman who fixed our dinner takes away what we could not eat. Her children will eat the rest. She returns with the tea. Her hands are large and calloused and red from the blood of the chicken. She sets the dented metal teapot on the ground and releases five glasses from her fingers.

It is almost dark now. Sori holds the teapot high above the ground and moves the ribbon of liquid from glass to glass without halting the flow. Not a drop is lost. The liquid falls into the small mouths of the glasses as if it could do nothing else.

There will be three shots of burning mint tea and three entreaties. It is a ritual, sacrosanct and pedestrian. It has been performed in every village we have passed through. In some villages we drank the tea when we arrived, in others as we departed. It is a ritual that recognizes that every welcome foreshadows a good-bye, every good-bye a welcome.

"To life." Sori raises his glass and we nod, looking into each other's eyes.

He waits for us to taste the sweetness.

In the morning Sori will have the women come down to the river with a cornucopia upon their heads and we will fill our hatches with blood oranges, green clumps of bananas, cassavas, dowels of sugarcane, bags of rice, tins of sardines.

Sori refills the glasses.

"To death." We nod to Sori and to each other.

Again he waits, the hot mint thick as syrup on our tongues.

Tomorrow children will carry our empty boats down to the river. The village will fall in behind them. It will be a high-spirited parade. We will slide our boats into the water and the children will hold them against the bank while we load them. They cannot be loaded on land. They are like whales, their frames cannot support the weight. They need the strength of water.

The children will hand us our paddles. As we glide away, the entire village will be crowded on the bridge waving and smiling. The old men and women, inured to the perpetual ebb and flow of life, holding their hands motionless in the air. The mothers waving the arms of their babies. The little girls turning their hands shyly. The boys so excited they will start shouting and begin once again hurling themselves off the bridge into the river.

Sori refills the glasses for the last time.

"To love," he says.

We clink our glasses and drink the sweet liquid.

The next day the river takes us away. We are drawn downstream swiftly. We look back and the bridge with all the little people grows small. We can't pick out Sori from the rest of the villagers. They are still waving but we can't hear them anymore.

We have swapped worlds: land for water. That which is rough and obdurate and predictable for that which is soft and viscous and fickle. They are two completely different elements and I know it and feel it in the very first moments of boating.

The river bends and we bend with it and we are alone on the Niger. Mike, me, John, Rick, in single file with great spaces of brown water between us.

The river is wide and flat. There are no waves, no rapids, no ripples; the water moving as one piece. A magic carpet.

My eyes roam from bank to bank. The river is tumescent, pouring through the trees, bending them over and tearing them out from their roots. Yet everything is hushed, still.

Too still, I think. As if the river has some secret but is holding its tongue. As if the river is only feigning placidity. Something is starting to happen but I don't yet know what it is.

I squint back at Rick and John. They are fine, cruising along. I look forward. Mike is ahead of me. He's sliding around the next bend. Just before he disappears he glances over his shoulder at me, raises his paddle and points downstream. He can see something we can't. He's grinning like a dog.

Moments later the current swings me around the bend and I see what Mike was pointing at.

Rick and John will think they were tricked, hoodwinked. They were afraid to put in at Dougelema. They wanted to go farther downstream where the river would be wider, calmer. They thought the water was still too fast, too dangerous, too unknown. And now it's too late.

Rick and John are swept out to my left. They see it. Rick stops paddling; so does John. Rick's mouth begins moving strangely. John's face goes gray.

Before us is a parapet, a gigantic wall of debris. We thought the river had bored out a course through the bush but it has not. In front of us is a towering dam of mangled trees and limbs and bushes and mud and grass, the whole thing bound up with roots and vines like some medieval battlement.

I hear Mike bellow and turn to watch him. He is stroking hard, galloping straight for the dark tangled wall like a knight in a jousting tournament. He's aiming for a hole. One last whoop and he crashes into the barricade and is swallowed.

I am backpaddling, searching for my own tunnel, but it's impossible. The river is dragging me into the rampart. I spot a tiny cave and aim for it, cutting the water with my paddle. Just as my bow goes under, I realize the hole is too small. I'm going to be decapitated. I snap forward, cramming my head and shoulders into the cockpit. Face to crotch I go ripping inside and then it's as if somebody is kicking my boat and everything is rushing and slamming one way then another and I hold tight but now branches are gouging my back and I twist and try to slip free but can't.

I sit up. I am in a flooding prison. Limbs are snatching at me from above and vines have wrapped around my hull and the current is pulling me sideways tipping me over. I have visions of myself entangled underwater, eyes bulging, kicking and fighting, my legs pinned in my kayak. I throw my hands over my head and reach for anything and pull up, lifting my boat out of the water. Without thinking I begin hauling myself forward through the maze, my bow cleaving curtains of interlaced leaves, the keel rocking, the hull scraping, black water catching me and throwing me and it's hell and I love it and then the web is spreading and my boat shudders and I give one final heave-ho and I'm out, gliding over open water in dazzling sunshine.

"*Yeessss!*"

I hear someone shouting.

". . . finest damn strainer I ever saw in my life."

Mike is playing in an eddy near the bank, spinning his boat in circles. I am covered with spiders and ants and bark. My boat is crowned with broken branches. There's a slender blue snake in my lap.

I paddle toward Mike, slip into his eddy and ram right into him. He roars with delight and whacks his paddle on the water and we proceed to howl and wrestle and soak each other.

After several minutes we start wondering where Rick and John are. We wait, and wait, and they don't show. We're just heading back in to look for them when they punch out of the sieve.

They both look bewildered, stunned. Rick is drenched. He must have tipped over.

John is livid. "This is too dangerous!"

Mike and I stare at each other, grinning stupidly. It's the wrong thing to do but we can't help it. I know John thinks we are imprudent. And impudent.

They paddle toward us slowly. John's face is pinched. Rick is dripping and pale and pie-eyed.

"This isn't boating!" John's voice is quivering with rage. It surprises me. I look at Mike.

Mike can't stop grinning. He turns to me and says quietly, "Nope. This is exploring."

I don't think Rick or John hear him. If they do they don't acknowledge it. They don't come in close either. They keep some distance.

Rick is beside John. He says, "I didn't come here for this."

John nods his head fiercely.

Nothing more is said. We are all left sitting dumb-faced in our pointy little boats in the lax brown water, our paddles laid across our cockpits. After a while we start down the river together again, no one speaking, each of us hiding out in his own thoughts.

I rewind, the way you do after a quarrel. Start at the bridge. Waving, paddling away, turning the bend, seeing the wall, fear, aiming, hitting, inside, fighting, joy, fighting, joy, escape.

I replay the exchange of words. The whole thing strikes me as odd. What you come for and what you get are almost always irreconcilable. That is the nature of travel. Rick and John have traveled. They know this.

So why are they so angry? I rewind even further. Back to America. Back to when we were planning the trip. We all knew the headwaters of the Niger were unknown and had never been navigated. We knew we didn't know what to expect—that was the reason we chose the Niger. We *wanted* not to know what to expect.

Gradually, I implode. For a moment it's like an epiphany, but then in the next second it's so obvious I can't believe I didn't see it from the beginning. Those were *our* reasons for this journey, Mike's and mine, not theirs.

Mike and I came to Africa to be what we are; Rick and John came here to escape who they were.

We haven't been on the river an hour, we aren't more than five miles downstream, and already our differences are insurmountable.

"Yaaahoooo!"

I snap to.

Mike is waving his paddle in the air like a kid with a cardboard sword. We have come around the next bend in the river; another wall lies dead ahead.

Shortly after Houghton's last note, rumors began seeping out of the jungle that he was dead. The African Association waited a year before announcing he was missing. Houghton's wife and children were dragged off to debtors' prison. Eventually, the association provided her with a pension and she and her children were released.

In 1795 a young Scotsman named Mungo Park stepped into the ring. As much for his ambition as for his accomplishments, Park was destined to go down in history as the most famous West African explorer. He expected no less.

Park was a robust, romantic, headstrong man who would set a precedent for stamina and tenacity. Son of a Selkirk farmer, he was the seventh of thirteen children. Apprenticed to a Scottish surgeon at fifteen he subsequently graduated from the medical school of Edinburgh University, took a position as a ship's doctor, and sailed to Sumatra. Upon his return he presented himself before the African Association and they took him at once.

His mission was the same as his predecessor's. This time, for the sake of safety, a fifty-man escort was to accompany the explorer. But Park was impatient and left before it was organized. He was twenty-four years old.

After acclimatizing to Africa—a six-month period of illness and fever—Park set out with a guide named Johnson, a slave, a horse, and two asses. He followed Houghton's trail. Like Houghton, he was forced to pay tribute in every fiefdom he passed through. He too gave up a waistcoat; the chief was taken with the shiny buttons. Another chief liked his umbrella. At other times he was simply robbed. The farther he penetrated into the land of the Moors, the more often he was spit upon, harassed, and abused. His guide, Johnson, abandoned him. Then, on the edge of the Sahara, he was taken prisoner by horsemen.

During captivity he was told he would have his hands chopped off, or be blinded, or executed. But the women of the chief's seraglio were attracted to him. His skin was so white, they said, he must have been dipped in milk as a child. They wanted to verify for themselves that infidels were circumcised. Park offered to show the prettiest of them, but she declined.

After two and a half months these women won his release. He marched on and was immediately robbed and left to die of thirst in the desert. A freak thunderstorm saved his life. He stripped off his rags, sucked the water out of them, and resumed his search for the Niger.

Ten months after leaving England, Mungo Park reached the Niger River at the city of Ségou. He fell to his knees, thanked God, and drank from the muddy river. Houghton had said the Niger flowed east; Park had proven it.

Gaunt and raw, his horse dead, and without means to hire a canoe, Park set out to follow the course of the Niger on foot. He got within four hundred miles of Timbuktu before the monsoon arrived. He was not a man to give in, but if he continued, he would die. He turned around.

His journey back to the west coast of Africa was no less brutal. Two and a half years after departing England, Mungo Park returned. He had been given up for dead. As the African Association's first successful explorer, he was lionized.

Sir Joseph Banks, still the prime force in the African Association, urged Park to write a book about his journey. *Travels in the Interior of Africa* was a powerful adventure tale told in plain English. It sold out in a week. Mungo Park was England's Odysseus.

But Africa had left him with a ruined stomach and feverish nightmares. He returned to Scotland and fell in love with the daughter of the surgeon he had once apprenticed under. They married, bought a house and Park went to work as a country doctor.

The river is two-faced, two-hearted for the next three days. Stretches of pious brown water; then you round the bend.

Mike and I look forward to every battle. We fly at the barricades together, paddles whirring, finding a hole only at the last moment and both shooting for it. Once inside we fight side by side laughing and slashing and hollering oaths.

Rick and John look forward to every interlude. They tackle each wall grim but resolute. Mike suggests I use the machete to hack out holes for them. It is a sword, so I have a grand time chopping away, but the palisades are so springy and ductile it makes no difference. Being a few centuries too late to really know what I'm doing, I eventually lose it. The blade lops off a limb too easily and the momentum plunges the weapon out of my hand and into the drink.

By the end of each day all four of us are scratched, bruised, and pleasantly exhausted. We pitch camp in the tall grass on the bank. The pure physicalness of the boating makes me and Mike rambunctious. One night we're clowning around and Mike throws me and I trip and crash onto our tent breaking the poles. We fix them with duct tape but the tent is a hassle to set up from then on. Rick and John don't say a word. Serves us right.

By the fourth day the walls are beginning to dwindle. The river has almost plowed a clean swath. John and Rick are relieved. Luckily there's something new to think about.

Crocs.

We rarely see them but we hear them. Thwacks on the water, then a gulping sound. John saw the first big one. He said it slithered down the bank and disappeared into the river. I passed below one the same day. It was stretched out on a limb on its stomach, legs dangling, eyes closed. It was five feet long. John says the one he saw was much, much bigger. Mike and I think it's time to get out the guns.

"We don't bother them, they won't bother us," says John.

"C'mon guys," says Rick. "Crocodiles? Millions of years old and not changed one iota? We're not part of their natural diet."

"That's the point," says Mike. "They survived because they aren't picky. Meat's meat. We're no different to a crocodile than any other animal floating down the river."

I tell Rick and John about the time in Zambia I met a boy missing a foot. He had a crude crutch and a hanging pant leg. His father told me they were fishing and a crocodile came right up into the boat.

Mike tells them about the time in South Africa he met a man with a horseshoe scar across his stomach.

"Looked like a zipper."

"Maybe those people provoked the crocodiles."

"Nope. Humans are a crocodilian delicacy," says Mike.

He points out how low we sit in the river and that it would require nothing more than a lazy, three-foot lunge to take our heads off. He says our paddles striking the water sound like an animal in distress to a crocodile. Instead of ignoring us, crocodiles will actually seek us out, come after us.

Rick and John shake their heads in dismay. I honestly don't know if Mike believes what he is saying or is just pulling our leg.

John asks me if I think I could really hit a crocodile.

"I'd try."

"Crocodiles aren't interested in us for dinner, period," states Rick. He says it so authoritatively it makes me wonder if he would put his body where his mouth is.

At lunch on the bank, eating bananas and slapping mosquitoes, Mike and I get out the Rugers and jack in full clips. We don't have holsters. The only way to carry them is between our legs lying on the hull of the boat. We tie lanyards to the grips and knot them to the chines inside our cockpits.

Back on the river paddling by myself I start to wonder whether I really could hit a crocodile. Crocodiles are fast. That's another reason they are the *über*lizard. I would have to see it coming. If a croc approached underwater and shot up from the depths it would take any one of us down before I could drop my paddle and grab the gun.

I am not a marksman. I grew up hunting elk, antelope, and deer so I'm a fair shot with a rifle, but a handgun is different. Mike and I practiced but not enough. To be good with a handgun you have to be very fast and accurate. I don't know how fast I am. If I don't know, I am not fast. If you have time, you use a rifle. Rifles are an offensive weapon. The weapon of the hunter. Handguns are for close quarters. They are a defensive weapon. If you're an intelligent hunter, you never get so close to your prey or your enemy that you need a handgun.

I have no moral problems killing an animal. Got over that hypocrisy a long time ago. It occurs to me that this may be John's real objection to the guns. Perhaps he was asking me not whether I could *hit* a crocodile, but rather if I could actually *shoot* one. Maybe this is Rick's thing as well. He is a pacifist. I remember when Mike and I were pacifists. We went through that together. It is an onanistic sophistry. As long as you only have yourself to look after, it works fine. But as soon as you love someone, and that someone is in danger, it goes right out the window. If it doesn't, your love is false, or you are a coward.

I stop stroking and stow my paddle and pick up the Ruger. I can feel its lethalness. You can feel it in all weapons. A mortal weightiness that makes them heavier than they actually are.

I am drifting by a half-submerged log. I hold the gun out with both hands, lock arms, close one eye, aim, sliding by, steady, steady. . . .

Click.

One morning I am on a straight stretch of river ahead of the others. I am not thinking about anything, just paddling. Moving my boat through the warm water. The river is dun, the banks verdant, the sky pallid blue.

For no reason I turn my head and glance over my shoulder.

Mike and John are backpaddling wildly, trying to shove their boats in reverse. Rick is halfway between me and them. He is perhaps forty feet behind me, gliding serenely through the water. To his right is a rippling wedge moving directly for him. Bulbous nose and slick eyes and then nothing for fifteen feet until the ridge of a notched, swaying tail.

Mike has stowed his paddle and is scrambling for his gun.

I drop my paddle and jerk on the lanyard. The gun pops into my hand. I swing around in my cockpit and brace my elbows on the combing and try to compose myself.

Rick is almost dawdling. The croc is coming right at him but he is not speeding up or slowing down, he is paddling languidly, now and again turning his head to watch the croc swimming toward him.

Mike has his gun in his hands and his shoulders blocked. His boat is sliding soundlessly toward Rick. John is behind Mike, frozen.

Twisted around, the 9-millimeter steady in both hands, consciously controlling my breathing, my arms slowly moving with the croc, watching Mike out of the corner of my eye with Rick between us and the crocodile going straight for him, I suddenly see what will happen. We will both fire at once and it will be like some slapstick shtick. I will kill Mike and Mike will kill me, and the croc, seeing his chance, will drag Rick under.

Rick is relaxed. I don't know if he's even noticed the rest of us.

The croc is closing in. Thirty feet, twenty feet, ten feet . . .

Blup.

The croc vanishes.

I wait, holding mortally still, finger on the trigger, aiming, expecting a primeval salamander to surge from the placid water, jaws clapping, teeth gnashing, and in one clean chomp take Rick's head right off.

Nothing. The river is blank.

Rick paddles past me, turns his head, and smiles.

We decide to travel in a convoy. Single file, a hundred feet between each kayak, the gunboats in positions one and three.

We make up signals: Paddle held horizontally overhead with hands equally spaced—stop. Paddle held vertically overhead—caution. Paddle held vertically overhead and waved—emergency, come quick. Paddle held horizontally overhead with blade extended to port or starboard—something is over there, look. Paddle held horizontally overhead and vigorously stroking the air—paddle hard, now.

Who knows if they will help.

Mike and I alternate as point man. We both want it. It is the chance to play scout.

Now that we are seriously looking for crocs, we see them. They are seldom out in the body of the river. They stay in the shade along the banks, their greasy green eyes peeping through the drowned trees.

When you are hunting, you don't look for shapes or colors. If you do, everything is an animal. Logs look like bodies, branches like claws, sticks like tails. Instead you learn to let your eyes ride over the landscape on their own. They will search for you. It is not form or hue they will pick out, but motion. Your eyes spot movement instinctively, even the breath of movement, and hold on it like a pointing dog until your mind sees what they see. It is evolutionary. The human nose is a joke, the ears barely adequate; but the *eyes*, the eyes of a human are the eyes of a predator.

It feels good to be hunting. The moment you begin to hunt, you cease being the hunted. It is a complete metamorphosis. To hunt is to believe in your own power, to believe you will win and not lose. It's a worthwhile feeling even when it doesn't work and you are defeated. And we all are defeated, just not by what we think will defeat us.

That night the sides of the river are so overgrown it's difficult to find a place to dock. It gets dark and we finally have to pull off right where we are. We thread through the sunken trees, jump into the black water, haul our boats through the mud, and tie up.

We tramp down a spot in a mangle of ferns and set up the tents by rote. John whips dinner together, something invisible at the bottom of the pot; then we repair to our separate tents like old couples. For a few minutes the beams of our headlamps roam the surface of our homes, seeking bugs. We kill all we can, click off our lights, lie back, and sleep.

We wake in the morning with backaches. Lumpy beds and too many hours in the saddle. We move slow, our bodies taking longer to wake up than we do. Mike and John are finished dressing first and wander down to the boats. Rick and I begin to drop our tents, sliding the poles out. Rick has his pants on, his shirt unbuttoned. I'm in shorts, no shirt.

I'm messing with the broken poles of our tent. My back is turned and I hear Rick start slapping—*thap, thap, thap*—but I'm not paying attention. Then he starts cursing, and Rick doesn't curse, and then a low rumble comes over me and Rick begins to screech. It's a piercing cry, a sound I have never heard a man make before. I spin around to find Rick twirling like a dervish slapping and screeching and then he is flying toward me passing me and I'm running now too not knowing what is happening until the black cloud is all around me stinging me and Rick is already in the water and John is in the water and I'm diving in.

I am underwater swimming. I can feel the creatures fluttering in my flesh like thorns. I swim out where the current is and come to the surface and grab the limbs to keep from being swept away and start pulling myself back in toward shore.

Rick and John are there. Only their heads stick above the water. As I come in, John shouts, "Duck!" and their heads disappear and then I see the patrol of bees and go under myself but start giggling and have to come up.

Seconds later Rick and John pop to the surface.

"Looked like they got you bad," says Rick.

"Did they get you?"

"Mostly on the head."

"Duck!"

Beneath the water we are safe. It is our carapace. But we can only hold our breath for so long. We come up together.

"Where's Mike?"

John points down the bank. Mike didn't go into the

water. He's standing stock-still, his hands clamped over his face, bees crawling all over him.

"Mike, you all right?"

"Just dandy." His voice is muffled.

Bees are everywhere. They are sending out patrol after patrol looking for us. We go under, hold our breath, come up.

"Rick, what happened?"

"Did you see the hive?"

"No."

"We camped right under it. Thing's big as a cage ball. It was hanging from that tree. I accidentally jabbed it with a tent pole."

We start laughing but our laughter gets garbled because we have to go under again.

When we come up, John whispers, "Look at the boats."

Our kayaks are carpeted with a fibrillating mass. We have been living on oranges and our nylon cockpits are soaked with juice.

Rick says, "We'll just have to wait it out."

We've been in the water half an hour when Mike moves. He takes one very slow step, then stops, his hands still over his face. Two minutes later he takes another step. In twenty minutes he has gone twenty feet.

The roar is subsiding now. The patrols are gone but our boats are still unapproachable. Rick and I are still hiding out in the water. John has pulled his shirt up over his head and has started moving toward the boats, staying as much under water as possible.

Mike is taking one slow step at a time along the bank. He has removed his hands from his face. Bees land, crawl across his cheeks, along his lips, over his eyelids, then fly away. We wait and watch.

We have been in the water over an hour when Mike reaches the boats. The decks are still heavy with bees. With a bare hand he slowly wipes the bees off the rear hatch. They plop into the mud in a yellow clump. He opens the hatch, pulls out his cap with the bug net, gently wipes the bees off his face and neck, puts the cap on and drops the net. He reaches back inside the hatch, lifts out a pair of leather gloves, slides his hands inside. He is safe. He stands up, turns to us and waves with both hands.

"Hi, guys."

We are incredulous. "Did you get stung at all?"

"Nope." He shakes his head and grins. "So, guys," suddenly he starts coughing with laughter, "how's the water?"

"What? What is it?"

"Forget about the crocs?"

We boat all day hardly speaking. The banks close in and we skim through dim passageways, peeping into the shadows.

When the jungle is all around us like this, almost on top of us, it doesn't feel as if we're moving downstream. It feels as if we're moving upstream, up into someplace dark and nepenthean.

We all jump when a troop of monkeys begins screaming. They are very large monkeys. They resemble furry, evil children. They screech and show us their sharp teeth and thrash through the trees trying to chase us away.

In the late afternoon we spot a dugout along the bank and pull off. It is filled with mud. There is a trail leading into the bush but it is so indistinct we don't know if it was made by humans or animals. We follow it hoping it will lead us to a village but it just burrows on and on until we have to turn around.

That night a heavy fog settles over us. In the morning we huddle together and eat the last of our food. Bananas turned bitter, hunks of cassava left in the pot from the night before. We whisper instead of talk as though the fog were a net that could drop on us if we raised our voices. John thinks we could make Faranah today. Rick hopes so. Mike doesn't think we can but that's only because he doesn't want to.

We load our boats in the thick mist and slide them like spoons into the blood of the water. We plan to travel in convoy but the fog separates us immediately. At first we call out to one another; then we stop, letting each of us find his own way. We can't get lost. We're on a river, not an ocean.

I let the current carry me, my prow spreading the petals of whiteness and pulling me through as if I were passing into the depths of a flower. I listen to the small joyful sounds my paddle makes upon the water.

Once I stop my arms and coast, the paddle clasped before me. I want to listen to the sound of my boat slipping through the water. I think I can hear it, but perhaps not.

Sometimes I think I see a shadow glancing through the void beside me. It comes and goes. Only when the fog begins to lift do I realize it is Michael. We have been parallel for a long time. We are bending in toward each other when he raises his paddle and points downriver.

There's something out there, a phantom. We line up and paddle together not knowing what it is we are pursuing. Then the veil lifts.

It is a man. He is lean, knotted with muscle, putting his shoulders into the pole. He is sending his dugout over the water like a gondolier with a message. Before we can get his attention he vanishes into the reeds.

We follow him. We find his boat but he is gone. We scramble up the bank and run through a tunnel of grass. At the end of the tunnel there is an opening.

Inside the enclosure there will be five blind men. The boatman and an old man with gray hair and three others. At their feet will be a drawing in the dirt. A circle with wavy lines inside it.

The men will be mute and rigid as animals. Rough dusty legs of muscle and bodies of muscle and inscrutable faces.

When we ask them questions, they will not respond to us. They will be blank. Human pillars supporting the weight of the African sky. Mike and I will go back to our boats. Out on the river we will slide into an eddy to wait for Rick and John and wonder why the old man drew a picture in the sand that none of them could see.

But it was not drawn for them. It was drawn for us.

On every journey there is something waiting for you. Something specific. When you find it, you will think it just happened to be there, but in fact it was there only for you. It is not a coincidence. If you had not found it, it would not have been there.

While Mungo Park was still in Africa, and at the time presumed dead, the African Association sent out another explorer, Friedrich Hornemann.

Hornemann was an intrepid, intelligent twenty-five-year-old German who had studied theology at Göttingen University. He got the assignment because one of his mentors was a friend of Sir Joseph Banks.

The African Association again shifted its focus to the northern approach. Hornemann was sent to Egypt. The French and the English were at war and shortly after his arrival Napoleon captured Alexandria at the Battle of the Pyramids. This delayed Hornemann's departure and he used the time to become fluent in Arabic. He also managed to get himself introduced to Napoleon. The general was so impressed by his courage he offered to provide him with a French passport, now a necessary travel document.

His stay in Egypt convinced Hornemann that the only way to travel safely and swiftly in Muslim countries was to become a Muslim. He decided to pose as a desert merchant.

During the first part of his journey he was called out on several occasions, but always proved himself one of the faithful by reading out loud from the Koran. The Sahara soon swallowed him. In his last letter to Banks, Hornemann said he was certain the Niger and the Nile were two different rivers.

It is not known when Hornemann reached the Niger, but he did, somewhere south of the great bend. He followed it to within three hundred miles of its terminus in the Gulf of Guinea before dying of dysentery.

Hornemann's death was not confirmed for another

117

twenty years. In the meantime the African Association published his journal, mailed a copy to Napoleon, and sent out another explorer, Henry Nicholls.

With the city of Timbuktu and the course of the Niger still an enigma, and having tried both the northern and western approaches, the Association sent Nicholls to the south. Nicholls arrived on the Gulf of Guinea in 1805 with orders to find the Niger and follow it to the end. Alas, he was beginning at the end. Of course he didn't know this. You never do. He died of fever in four months.

While Hornemann and Nicholls were perishing on the banks of the Niger, Mungo Park was growing bored and restless in Scotland. Banks made him an offer he couldn't refuse. If he would lead another expedition into Africa, he would be given the rank of captain and the full sponsorship of the British government. Banks promised Park it would be a military expedition composed of stout, well-trained, well-equipped soldiers.

On his first journey Park was a resourceful, resilient, reasonably understanding man. But it had been a harsh adventure and the years in Scotland mulling it over had changed him. He returned to Africa with the mind-set of a conqueror and the blindness of an avenger.

His expedition was composed of forty-four men—Park, thirty-four soldiers bribed off a ship with the promise of double pay, five convicts who were also carpenters and expected to build a boat when they reached the Niger, three officers, one of whom was his brother-in-law, and an African guide named Isaaco.

Park headed inland from the west coast in 1806. He was full of confidence and vainglory and marched his men right into the monsoon season. The first soldier died of an epileptic seizure. The next of dysentery. A bee attack killed six donkeys and one horse. Isaaco the guide was attacked by a crocodile and saved himself only by gouging his thumbs into the animal's eyes. He was left with deep wounds on both thighs. Soldiers began to collapse or go mad from a multiplicity of diseases. At first Park made valiant attempts to help his men. He loaded and unloaded the asses single-handedly, treated the sick, found enough food for his troops in each new village. At one river crossing he forded and reforded the stream sixteen times carrying soldiers on his back. Park may have been indefatigable, but his men were not. They kept dying.

By the time he reached the Niger thirty-three men had lost their lives. The carpenters were dead, but Park still managed to construct a forty-foot, flat-bottom schooner. By the time it was completed, three more men had died, including his brother-in-law. But nothing would stop him now. He dispatched Isaaco with his journal and letters to his wife and the African Association, hoisted the British flag, and set sail on the unknown Niger.

Not another word was ever heard from Mungo Park.

Two years later Isaaco was sent back into the African interior to find out what had happened.

Park had expected trouble. He had armored his vessel with bull skins and provisioned himself with fifteen muskets and considerable ammunition. Because he refused to stop and pay tribute while passing through each new kingdom along the river, his boat came under constant attack. He literally fought his way down the Niger. He managed to reach Timbuktu's port city of Kabara but could not dock, having made so many enemies. He continued downstream, exploring the course of the Niger. Past Timbuktu he had more difficulties. Attacks from hippos, attacks from Tuaregs. He shot his way through. Somewhere farther downstream, where the Niger squeezed into a narrow channel and cut through a band of rocks, Park was ambushed and killed.

Reaching Faranah is like a homecoming. We glide quietly beneath the bridge from which we first glimpsed the river, all the foreboding long since gone. We have run the upper headwaters of the Niger.

We pull into the reeds beside the bridge and slide our

boats out of the water. Mike and I walk up the road while John and Rick watch the boats. It feels odd to walk again after so much paddling. It was a hundred hard river miles from Dougelema to Faranah.

The Olafsons are so surprised to see us it makes me wonder whether they didn't actually believe we would perish. John immediately brings out the cold beer; Margot starts preparing dinner. Mike and I stroll back down the road with celebratory brews for Rick and John. Rick inspires several dozen children to carry our boats to the compound. He leads the throng up the hill like the Pied Piper. The gates swing open and then are quickly shut and the dirt kids remain on the other side looking through the bars and we have left Africa as simply as if we had boarded an airplane.

We are thinner than we were. Sunburned and scraped and welted from the bees. When we slip into the Olafsons' home, the shade instantly salves our crimped eyes. Cool air envelopes us; in our mouths it feels carbonated. We sink into chairs. The chairs are so soft we could lose consciousness in them. The beers are so rich they spill through our bodies like morphine, a new one pushed into our hands the moment the previous one is empty. We tell our tales and get thoroughly smashed. When dinner is ready, we sit down at a sparkling dining table and try to remember table manners while Margot ladles out homemade bean soup. After dinner we open the sliding door and step wobbly outside. The hot air and the sun hit us. We had forgotten about them. We weave over to the pool. There is a whitewashed picnic table beneath a trim canopy. The four of us stand in the circle of shade and drop off our smelly clothes and slip into the pool naked.

The water is ineffable. We sit in it with beers in our hands. The bottles drip. How did they get this beer so cold? Really, it's impossible. And this swimming pool, it's so clean. How'd they do that? Where's the muck? Leaves and shit? Where are the bugs? We don't see one goddamned bug. *Christ*, this is the life! Why would anyone live any other way?

We are in shock. We recognize it but we are too drunk

not to enjoy it. Africa is a thousand miles away. Our journey down the Niger seems unreal to us, as if we had read about it in some adventure book. The hike to the headwaters must have been at the beginning of the book because it seems so far away we can hardly recall it. Remember Sori? Sori Keita. He was our guide, right? Remember villages and chiefs? Remember dancing in the moonlight?

We jabber nonsense until it gets dark, then heave ourselves out of the pool and sleep dead as corpses on the manicured gravel.

People talk about culture shock as a temporary disorientation when you go from someplace you know to someplace you don't. Or when you go from someplace where you know you can have almost anything you want to someplace where it's hard just finding food and shelter. But it's far more disorienting to go the other way. Your senses are suddenly gushing, as if everything has become incontinent at once. Going from prodigality to austerity you act rationally. Suck it in, cinch up your belt, do what you have to do. Going the other way you lose it right off the bat.

Decadence is that seductive. It can make you soft in a matter of days. Not your body, your mind. It's like the devil whispering in your ear. Makes you question what the hell you were doing in the first place. What was the point? What river? Now who really gives a shit. Listen too closely and you can lose your focus.

Fortunately, after you've surfeited yourself a few times, the whisper grows faint and you pull your head out and remember why you came and make plans to get on with it.

We stay in town just long enough to have a couple of good drinks and resupply: then we're back on the Niger.

Beyond Faranah the river grows fat. Fat and lazy. Got itself down out of the mountains and now it's taking it easy, sprawling out.

The barricades across the river have been gone for days.

Not even a raft of busted-up trees to paddle around, maybe climb up on and get a view of the countryside. The crocs are gone as well. They stay near the banks where the hunting is better. We're clear out in the middle of a river as wide as a lake.

Rick and John are delighted. This is what they came for. A big broad river lolling in syrupy loops across the African savanna. Endless flatwater. They lean back and paddle peacefully and enjoy the hell out of it.

Mike and I try not to get bored. Flatwater is what we dreaded. We knew from the start the Niger didn't have much of a drop but we thought going at the end of the rainy season might help. And it did. Up high the water was running narrow and fast. But it was only gravity that gave the river impetus. Now that the landscape has flattened out, the urgency is gone and the river has lost its speed. Once the water was racing at ten miles per hour; now it's down to one or two. And those are river miles, not map miles.

River miles are like trail miles. Our maps show an ample floodplain with a river inside it. The outline of the floodplain is accurate enough but the course of the river inside is pure speculation. The river is in a constant state of flux, different every year, every month, every day. It never runs straight. There are no straight lines in nature. Straight lines are the creation of a mathematical imagination. The Niger is herniated with oxbows, as kinked as your intestines.

We have dropped into dry country. The rain that fell in the mountains does not fall here. The dirt is tan or even yellow, not black. You can see it in the cutbanks. The air is different too. Dry as kindling, scentless, opened up above us like a house with its roof blown off.

John begins to watch for birds. He is a birdwatcher, an amateur ornithologist. I did not know this. At lunch he will describe the birds he saw. Their colors, their behavior.

Interesting disclosures about John keep emerging. How every time we're around kids he'll find a scrap of paper and transform it into a beautiful creature and give it to them.

How his wry sense of humor bounds out at the perfect moment. How he has become the team chief.

Rick told me that once, when he and John were bicycling in Tibet, they passed a man savagely flogging his mule and John leapt off his bicycle and wrenched the club from the man's hand and threatened to hit him with it if he did not stop.

As for Rick, the indolence of the river has turned him back into his old affable, eloquent self—the sedulous conversationalist. I start boating with him more and more. We spend hours on the same old subjects: the meaning of life, death, dialectic, art, community. It keeps my mind occupied, makes the miles go down easier.

Mike will paddle in, listen for a few minutes, then paddle away. Our elliptical prattle bores him. Talk, just to be talking, is the cheapest thing imaginable to Mike. He believes in action. He loves discourse, but it must go somewhere. To Mike the point of discourse is to define the problem and develop a set of potential solutions. Then execute. Execution is everything. He has spent his adult life doing just this. World hunger. Economic development in African villages. Running a program for disadvantaged families in Wyoming.

Rick is just the opposite. To Rick talk is priceless. He is a Bohemian. He doesn't believe he can do any more than be what he is, which is a man who doesn't believe he can do any more than be what he is. Rick thinks that because he admits he is not doing anything, it absolves him of the obligation.

One day we raft up together, hooking our paddles across each other's boats, and Rick begins expanding on his idea of the perfect community.

It must be a small place, of course. Familial. A few coffee shops. Everybody walks or rides a bicycle. Everybody listens to music or better yet makes their own. Everybody has the time to develop themselves creatively. Lots of village bonhomie. A nice little Left Bank kind of place.

"Sounds great, Rick."

He nods. He's still hoping to find such a place along the Niger. The promised land, just around the next bend.

"Faranah was a nice place."

"Yes it was."

"They even had a disco."

"That was incredible, wasn't it."

The night before we got back on the Niger, Rick and I stayed out dancing till three in the morning.

"What'd you think about those kids?"

"Man, they can dance!"

"No, the other ones."

He knows what I'm talking about. We were told this story several times in Faranah by several different people:

A twelve-year-old boy stole a sack of rice. His father had abandoned the family and his brothers and sisters had no food. They didn't know how he did it because the sack of rice was twice as heavy as he was. He climbed through the window in a storage building and lifted the sack up to the opening and pushed it out. Then he jumped through the window and somehow got the sack on his back and started carrying it home. But the sack was too heavy for him. So he hid it beside a building and went to get a friend to help him. Between the two of them, side by side bent over with the sack crosswise on their backs, they could walk. They don't know how the boys got the sack up on their backs. But the sack had a hole in it. The villagers followed the trail of rice and spotted the two boys. The boys tried to run but they couldn't with the sack on their backs. They dropped the sack and fled but the villagers caught them. The boys pleaded. The villagers killed the two boys. Beat them to death with stones and iron bars.

"It's sick," says Rick.

I ask him if he has ever been attacked.

"No." He says he hasn't ever done anything to warrant being attacked.

"Has Mike told you about what happened in the Transkei?"

"No."

"Ask him sometime."

Mike and Diana were attacked in the night in South Africa by an unknown number of assailants. They escaped, but were then tracked. Had Mike not done some good thinking, actual strategizing defenses, he and Diana would have been killed.

"And I told you about what happened to Sue and me."

Rick knows this story. On a bicycle trip in Yugoslavia, Sue and I were attacked at night in our tent. The assailants kicked and beat us inside our tent before slashing it open with a knife. There were four men. I was out of my mind and came out screeching and slashing with a six-inch blade and they ran off.

"I guess I've just been lucky." Rick doesn't like these stories. "I haven't even had that many things stolen. My bike in Mexico and those shoes."

Someone had pinched Rick's shoes on our last night in Dougelema. He had left them outside the hut in full view of an entire village of shoeless people. He'd gotten the shoes for free from Mike's sponsorship work and he still had his sandals, so I thought he would just blow it off, say something like, "Oh well, guy probably needed them more than I do."

But he didn't. He had been upset. Angry. He wanted to catch the thief.

After we got bored with the beach we packed up and continued south, but we didn't get far. A war stopped us in Spanish Sahara.

It was a war no one but the participants knew about. Throats cut. Men sitting against mud walls with their eyes open and holes in their heads. Piles of bloated camels. Starving children. We didn't know what they were fighting for or against. We tried to persuade the soldiers to let us through. They raised their machine guns and told us if we didn't turn around they would shoot us.

We veered east into Algeria, traveling along the northern edge of the Sahara searching for another route to

Timbuktu. In a one-well village scalded by the sky a ruffian snatched my hat off my head and ran. Without the hat the sun would scalp me. I went after him and he turned on me with a dirk and I let him keep it.

A shirt drying on a bush disappeared. A water bottle and tin cup vanished at a putrid well. A sleeping pad, a sock, a stove that was broken anyway. The longer we traveled, the lighter our packs became. The desert was gradually dispossessing us of our possessions. We did not replace what was stolen. We learned to live without it.

And it was not only our belongings that were being pared down, but our bodies as well. I got bitten by a scorpion and we set up our tent in the burning sand beneath a shadeless thorn tree while I shivered through the fever. Mike got something in his stomach so rough he couldn't walk for two days. I got an infection in my foot that oozed red pus. We didn't have any drugs and the villagers had worse afflictions than we did. We ate what they ate and got their diseases. Our limbs lost their white-bread-and-beef American muscle. Eventually we became as lean as the jackals we heard howl at night out in the dunes.

It was spring. The sand burned right up through our boots. Mike, being a redhead, got so sunburned his skin cracked. We tried traveling at night but we couldn't sleep during the day because of the heat. We began dreaming of the ocean. We couldn't remember why we had left. We were plagued by visions of cool blue water. We started talking about water as we once talked about sex. In our minds, water became something sentient, sensual, erotic.

One afternoon we were trudging south on an ephemeral gravel road when Mike stopped in his tracks, wiped his face with his neckerchief, and slowly turned in a circle. We were surrounded by desert.

"Buck, we're frying."

We were. We were like two tiny insects out in the middle of an immense aluminum frypan.

"You know we have lots of time. All kinds of time."

"What do you mean?"

126

"I mean Timbuktu ain't going anywhere."

That was all it took. We turned 180 degrees.

As if the ocean were a magnet, we were sucked due north to the Mediterranean coast. For one whole day all we did was roll about in the water, rejoicing in the sheer voluptuous pleasure of liquid.

We started traveling eastward along the Algerian coast, beach to beach. One evening we made camp in Roman ruins on a bluff above the sea. We hid our tent in a thicket of thornbushes and left our sleeping bags and all our gear inside. There was a cool breeze coming off the ocean so we slipped on our jackets before loping down into a nearby village.

We would have stayed out late but just after dark I started feeling uneasy. I had a knot in my stomach and I didn't know why.

As I got older and kept traveling, I would learn to recognize this peculiar anxiety. It was a warning signal, an internal fire alarm. It was never mystical or fuzzy. I got a special kind of gut ache and knew something was wrong. It could wake me from a dead sleep. It is the kind of thing rational people scoff at, but over the years it would keep me from being robbed, even killed, more than once. I would learn to act immediately, without hesitation or fear, whenever I felt it.

But this was the first time and I didn't know what it meant or what to do. We were sitting in a cafe trying to get the attention of two women who unfortunately recognized us for what we were: boyish, ragged, and unkempt.

"Mike, something's wrong."

He grinned. "You're right. They're ignoring us."

"No, I mean I don't feel right."

"You sick?"

"No, it's not like that. Something's wrong."

"What are you talking about?"

"I don't know. I just feel weird."

Mike made me laugh with some wisecrack about how I should feel weird because I was a weird guy.

"I think we should head back to camp."

The women were slipping out the door without even looking at us.

Mike shrugged.

We left the cafe and walked through the village and started up the hill. As we drew closer to our camp, I began to feel increasingly anxious. Soon I was running. Mike was running beside me. We shot to the top of the hill and raced through the ruins into the bushes and before we even reached camp I knew we were too late.

The tent was gone. We went into shock immediately. We raged through the thornbushes in the dark screaming and cursing and bellowing threats. We kicked and punched at empty shadows, scratching the hell out of ourselves. After about an hour of this nonsense we slumped down in the moonlight with our backs against one of the stone pillars.

"We're idiots."

"We are. Absolute idiots."

"Dumb shits."

"Dickheads."

"Retards."

"Halfwits."

"Quarterwits."

"Hey, now that's going a little too far."

We started snickering, then howling, holding our sides.

We had lost everything. Our tent, our sleeping bags, our backpacks, clothes, cameras, film, you name it. All we had left were our jackknives, our money belts, and the clothes on our backs.

We fell asleep talking about all the gruesome things we would do to somebody if we happened to run into them on the street and they were wearing Mike's Boy Scout backpack, which he got in junior high, or shooting my 110 camera, which I bought in tenth grade for six dollars.

In the morning when we awoke, birds were chirping and the sky was baby blue and we sat up and got our backs against the pillar and looked around rubbing our eyes.

"Beautiful day."

"Perfect."

We had finally been released from the burden of possessions. Now we could travel.

The river becomes so large we no longer boat close
together. I begin paddling along the banks. It's more interesting than out in the emptiness of the river. There are
things to look at. A heron on a limb, sometimes a crocodile,
maybe a monkey. Yesterday I paddled along the left-hand
bank; today it is the right-hand shoreline.

I have been watching the land slide by for several hours
when I spot a gap in the foliage. It's a wide muddy patch.
Looks like a place where trucks have ground down to the
river.

But there aren't any trucks for hundreds of square miles.
I angle in to investigate.

I'm gliding straight for shore, the bank not thirty feet
away, when it dawns on me and I deftly reverse my stroke.
I've got my boat stopped and almost moving backward
when eight knobs appear on the surface of the water. Four
eyes, four ears. I keep retreating, ignoring the noise of my
heart, backing away from the two submerged hippos out
into the middle of the river and everything seems to be
going fine when suddenly I hear stomping and then a roar
and a hippo the size of a garbage truck comes crashing
through the trees shaking its mammoth head flopping its
mammoth mouth thrusting its pointed tusks. The hippo
plunges into the water and is swimming right for me and the
other two appear to be following him but I've already spun
on a dime and am flying for the opposite bank.

Rick and John and Mike must have come up behind me.
They are ahead of me now and we're all spreading out,
hightailing it across the river. I look over my shoulder
several times and each time it seems as if the hippos are
gaining. The last few hundred yards I don't look back. I'm
paddling so furiously my bow is bouncing off the water like

a motorboat. My prow plows into the bank and I catapult from the cockpit up into the bushes.

Stop. Look around. Rick is taking off through the bush. John is hiding behind a tree. Mike. Where's Mike! I spin around and peer at the river through the bushes. I can't see the hippos.

No. *No!*

I start running along the bank trying to get a good view of the river. I'm scrambling along the edge peeking out wherever there's a hole. I pass into head-high elephant grass still running looking sideways scanning the mendacious river thinking, *No not Mike, not Mike*, and trip right over him.

He's sitting in the grass with his feet dangling over the water looking through his binoculars.

"Mike!"

"Hey there."

"What are you doing!"

"Watching the hippos."

I sit down beside him. He hands me the binos and I glass the water. The hippos are not there for a while. Then they come up, then they go under. Each time they surface they are farther upstream.

"They weren't chasing us?"

"Lost interest."

"What are they doing?"

"Grazing upstream."

Over the next two weeks we don't see many hippos. Not nearly as many as we would like. The river is just too big.

Day after day the Niger continues to amass itself, convincing the new troops that they're going home to the open arms of the sea when in fact they are marching right into the desert. We pass where the Bale flows in, then the Oulinbe, the Biri, the Koba, the Koa Doula. With each infusion the river grows wider and slower.

We boat from eight in the morning until six in the evening. We see no one, not a soul. We are in a wilderness. We think we're making around thirty miles a day but we don't really know. We can't tell. We just paddle, hour after hour after hour, moving like robots down the flat river.

Every night we camp on the bank. We have a system. I put up our tent, Rick puts up theirs, John starts dinner, and Mike pumps water.

Dinner is something cooked and something fresh. We loaded up in Faranah. Bags of rocky rice, tins of sardines, tins of tomato paste, yams, a sack of hot peppers, hundreds of oranges and bananas. John squats in the grass and labors over two tiny gas stoves.

We drink the Niger to slake our thirst. At the source we drank it straight but thereafter it was muddy and we started pumping it through our filters. Now the river is so laden with silt it is like watery pudding. Mike and John and Rick continue to use their filters; I have given up. I scoop the Niger into my water bottle, spill in a few drops of iodine, wait half an hour, drink. The filters strain out the sediment and make the water look more appetizing, but what can harm you is too small to see.

We're exhausted, physically and mentally, by the end of each day. Sometimes we talk late into the night; just as often we don't, either because we're too tired or because we're tired of each other. We might listen to the shortwave, sitting around it as if it were a campfire, but we switch it off after a few minutes to save the batteries. Then we stand up, say good-night, and go to our tents.

I don't know what Rick and John do in their tent. Inside ours, Mike reads the Koran and I write in my journal. He is a Christian intrigued by Muslims. I am an infidel to both. We lie on our sleeping bags and sweat. In our ears, just beyond whatever we are trying to concentrate on, is the incessant threnody of the bugs. They grind their teeth all night long. They shove their sharp proboscises through the netting and whine for blood.

When Mike falls asleep, the Koran over his face, I light a

candle. I drip the wax onto the tent floor and stick the candle in the puddle and continue in my journal. After I've finished, I get out the maps and try to figure out where we are.

On the river we have no perspective. We are too close to the earth. Sunk in boats sunk in the water, all we can see is the blue expanse above us and the brown liquid all around us and the faraway green lines of the banks. It is a land-markless landscape. The only clue that we are passing through giant oxbows is the sun twirling dementedly above our heads.

I search the maps every night, attempting through sheer will to bring forth some form of relief. A gorge, a canyon, rapids, anything to break the mind-devouring monotony.

Early one afternoon bedrock rises up out of the middle of the river and my heart soars. We pull in to the great hump, moor our boats, and scamper about the island like cast-aways who have just been saved. Rick suggests we camp right here, right on this rock in the river.

It is the best campsite of the journey. We are surrounded by gurgling water. Sometimes it even seems to laugh. Our island is slit down the middle by a runner. We erect one tent on either side, opposite ends of the island. We each have our own space, our own view. Warm water races through the slit and we take turns bathing in it, sitting neck deep in the folds of stone, then lying naked on the hot rock.

That night Mike and I gab for hours.

"Mark, what kind of water do you think these boats can do?"

"Whitewater."

"No way."

"Back in the thirties, before plastic, the Germans were running rivers all over the world in skin boats. I got a book on it."

"Class III in foldables."

"At least."

I tell him about the pictures of pretty *Mädchens* in halter tops shooting rapids and hard men in tank tops slaloming gates.

"But I bet their boats weren't sixteen feet long and loaded with fifty pounds of gear."

We are all on the river by seven. It's running faster than it has for over a week, slicing down through the earth. Mike and I can hardly control ourselves. He is like the Tin Woodman come back to life, swiftwater a gift good as oil. I'm the Scarecrow, cut down from the cross of boredom. We dance and skip over the water, Dorothy and the Cowardly Lion right behind.

Within two hours the channel has narrowed and straightened and the river is running faster still. Suddenly there are obstacles. Sculpted stone islands, boulders, blocks the size of houses, all with white rapids spilling between them. Mike and I scoot through the holes and surf the ripples and wheel in the eddies. We get so far downstream we almost forget about Rick and John. At the head of a large rock island that splits the river into two channels, we pull off and wait.

Rick and John ride up shortly. We all get out of our boats and stand together on the highest point of the rock and look downriver. The right-hand channel is direct and fast, the left-hand channel circuitous and slow. When we climb back in our boats, Rick and John go left, Mike and I go right.

Immediately the water is tipping me and Mike through a funnel. We sweep around a bend and another and another and then we hear it. We know what it is and it sounds small enough so we keep paddling. We dart around a boulder and skate over a flat section and then it's right in front of us and below us and Mike is pulling off to scout and I zip past him and raise my paddle over my head and lean back and shoot over the falls.

It's only a ten-foot drop but as I hit the pool I hear my boat snap. I'm ejected out of the cockpit and slammed underwater. I hold on to my paddle and come up gasping and grab my boat and start swimming with it in my arms. I hear Mike yelling and I shout back but the falls are roaring and I'm being swept downstream. I push and frog-kick and eventually guide the wreckage of my boat through a cleft in the bushes.

My feet hit land. I am on a small sandbar in the middle of a swirling dark pool surrounded by walls of foliage. Perfect croc country. I bend over with my head near the water and turn in a circle peeping into the shadows. Can't see a damn thing. I reach under my boat. The Ruger is hanging by its lanyard in the water. I fish it out, raise it over my head, and pull the trigger to see if it's still working. It fires. I shove it into my pants.

My boat is doubled in half as if punched in the stomach. I pry it open and assess the damage. All the ribs and chines are broken, snapped in two right at the cockpit. Somehow the combing was not ruined. It must have popped out with me.

The boat is too heavy to move. I begin emptying the hatches. I know I have lost things but I don't know what. They floated away like entrails while I was trying to save the boat. I unload what's left, stacking it in the sand. When the boat is empty, I roll it over, stretch it out, squat down in the water, get under it, and stand up. Enough water spills out that I can drag it up onto the sandbar.

I have three pieces of metal tubing strapped inside the prow—the mast of a kayak sail. I cut two beams out of the trunks of two bushes and use them as pry bars to put the boat in traction. I remove the broken pieces of ribs and then splint the keel and the two chines, lashing the mast tubes to the broken ends first with wire, then nylon webbing, then duct tape. The cockpit is misshapen and I have to force the combing back in.

The repairs take two hours. Several times while I'm working I hear the telltale whack of a tail on the water, straighten up, whip out my gun, and slowly turn in a circle.

After I've done what I can do, I shove the boat across the sand and back into the water. It floats, although it's bent like a banana. I open the hatches and load what's left of my gear, then slip into the boat. I place the gun on my lap, yank the paddle out of the sand, and push off.

The boat no longer runs straight. It pulls hard to port. The rudder won't make up the difference. To compensate I must paddle two strokes on the right side for every one on the left. It's also leaking badly.

I navigate through channels overhung with vines, eventually returning to the main course of the river. Some distance downstream I find Mike and Rick and John on an island waiting for me. By now my boat is sinking.

They help me drag it up onto the rock and we unload it again and dump out the water and roll her over. The broken ribs punctured the hide. John solemnly gets out the patch kit. I sand the holes, cut out the rubber patches, apply the glue and press on the patches.

Then we all sit down and wait for the glue to dry. There are hundreds of bees buzzing around us but we have learned to ignore them, even when we are stung. Silently staring at the river, I am waiting for the inevitable. Eventually John can't hold it in any longer.

"Well. Was it worth it?"

The year is 1806. Ledyard, Houghton, Park, Hornemann, Nicholls—all of them were dead and the course of the Niger and the city of Timbuktu still conundrums.

Lewis and Clark had just returned from their epochal journey. Napoleon was conquering Europe, having brilliantly defeated the Austrians and Russians at the Battle of Austerlitz. The African Association was in decline, its tireless leader, Sir Joseph Banks, in a wheelchair and occupied with other duties. No one would have the strength of character to succeed him and the African Association would eventually be absorbed by the Royal Geographical Society. The exploration of Africa was taken up by the British government.

In 1815, Major John Peddie was sent to West Africa. He was to conscript a hundred men from the Royal Africa Corps. He died upon arrival. Peddie was replaced by Captain

Thomas Campbell. Bee attacks weakened Campbell's expedition and they made little progress before turning back. Then Campbell died. He was replaced by a man named William Gray and a military surgeon named John Dochard. Gray was captured by an avaricious chief but later rescued. Dochard and eight men reached the Niger between Bamako and Ségou, but the king of Ségou was suspicious and would not let them continue. Dozens upon dozens of men died in all this and no new information was obtained.

Captain James Kingston Tuckey was sent up the Congo River in 1816. Perhaps the Niger flowed into the Congo? No one knew. The heart of Africa was still sealed. There were fifty-three men in Tuckey's expedition, including five scientists. Only nineteen returned home. Tuckey was not one of them.

In 1818, Joseph Ritchie, George Lyon, and John Belford were sent south from Tripoli. Ritchie was a Scottish doctor who swung radically from profligacy to penury (the team set out with trunkloads of cork to preserve insects but no money to bribe chiefs). Lyon was a young, sensible navy officer. Belford was a shipwright; it was his task to build a boat when they reached the Niger.

Ritchie died of a bilious disorder in the desert. Lyon and Belford made it back alive, never having been within a thousand miles of the Niger or Timbuktu.

In 1822, Major Dixon Denham, Scotsman Hugh Clapperton, and naval surgeon Walter Oudney were sent out from Tripoli. A more dysfunctional team could not have existed. Denham was a priggish, small-minded autocrat; Clapperton, an overly proud giant of a man who had proven himself in the Napoleonic Wars; Oudney, a good country doctor. A sandstorm of recriminations blinded the expedition from the beginning. Denham was paranoid about his Scottish partners and snapped orders. They were rugged Scotsmen and told him to go to hell. Soon Denham and Clapperton were not speaking. In the middle of the Sahara their menservants ran vituperative, handwritten notes between the two men's tents. In hopes of permanently debilitating Clapperton, Denham began a rumor that Clapperton was a homosexual. For pre-Victorian men, there was no more scurrilous accusation. Clapperton was thunderstruck. They both fired off indignant letters of explanation to the British government. These missives were hand-carried across the flaming desert by two couriers, one expected to die en route.

Still, the expedition pushed on. They crossed the Sahara and ran up on the shores of unknown Lake Chad. Perhaps the Niger never did escape the continent? Perhaps it simply disappeared into this inland lake. Denham and Clapperton split up to explore the region; Oudney went with Clapperton. After covering the southern portions of the lake and discovering no substantial river, Clapperton and Oudney struck out west. Denham had already absconded north, joining a raiding party of two thousand horsemen intent on taking slaves.

It was the rainy season. Clapperton and Oudney fell ill with malaria and decided to wait it out. When they started moving again, it was winter. Water was freezing in the skin bags. Clapperton was barely alive. Oudney was worse. He had tuberculosis and died abruptly, trying to mount his camel. Clapperton struggled on, but was eventually stopped by warring tribes. Denham's slaving expedition was routed and he was almost killed by Fulani tribesmen.

Both Clapperton and Denham returned to Lake Chad and managed to survive another crossing of the Sahara. After three and a half years in the interior of Africa, they limped back into Tripoli and sailed to England together.

Neither of them ever found the Niger or Timbuktu. Denham spent the rest of his life resting on his thorny laurels, venomously attacking Clapperton. Clapperton, like so many great explorers, resolved to return to Africa.

When we first see the bridge, it is so far away it doesn't seem real. Perhaps it is a mirage. A quarter-mile-long cage set forty feet above the water, monuments of concrete dividing the river into equal parts. But as we slowly draw near, it doesn't disappear.

We begin to see movement. On shore, in the shade beneath the bridge, we make out naked boys. They are striking the water with sticks and splashing each other. One boy spots us and points. The others stop hitting the river and stare out at us, holding their sticks on their heads like spears.

When we finally glide in, the boys leap into the river and struggle out to us, the brown water up to their chests.

According to our maps, this is Kouroussa. Mike and Rick and John will go into town for food; I will stay with the boats. We drag their kayaks up the bank. They get out their daypacks and money and go off.

I'm left with the boys. They are wildly inquisitive. Rolling their eyes and jabbering, their small hard hands touching everything. As if boys emit a smell, like winged insects, new boys eager and reckless come tripping over themselves flying down the bank. I must make it clear that they can't play with the three beached boats. They are disappointed; instead they surround mine. They touch it, running their fingers along the ribs, fiddling with the deck lines, knocking heads to peer inside the cockpit. They are mechanically minded. They want to know how it works.

I was a boy once. It is a bright day and I have a long wait. I take up my paddle and slip back into my boat. I cleave the crowd standing in the water, paddle back out into the openness of the river and make two circles.

As I slide back in, I hold out my paddle. A dozen hands grab it. I sit in the boat and study all the boys pressed against the hull. They are so excited they are hostile. Eyes and elbows and fists, shouldering and twisting and fighting. I choose a small boy. All I can see is his head at water level between their legs. He squeezes through and I lift him onto my lap.

I stroke the boat around in a small circle near the shore. The boy is so proud. He keeps looking back at his friends and shouting to them and waving his arms. I let him hold the paddle with me but he is not paying attention. He doesn't notice the movement of the boat or the movement of the water. He is on stage, like a dancer, his eyes on his audience and his head held in place until his neck can twist no more and he must spin it around.

I don't know if I have done the right thing. I paddle the boat back into the gang of boys. They are insolent with envy and desire. I choose another child, lift him in, backpaddle out.

I give rides for an hour. The boys are beside themselves with pride and power and happiness.

Circling back in with what I have decided is my last passenger, I see a girl coming down to the river. The bank is steep and slick. She is careful, stepping through the web of tree roots as if they were hands that could grab her. On her head she is balancing an enormous basin.

When I lift the last boy out, others are fighting to get in. I push the mob back and step out of the boat and stand on a rock. Several boys start to get into my boat and I yell at them. One ignores me and climbs into the cockpit and I am forced to haul him out. He is indignant and tries to hurt me with his eyes.

I am watching the girl. Perhaps she is eight years old. She is walking with her neck. Her neck is lean and long. Her shoulders are narrow and square and her head does not turn. The basin floats through the air. Her grace is effortless and shocking.

As she descends the slope, I see feet protruding from the sides of her waist. By her walk and her shoulders it is plain she has been carrying this child since he was born. Perhaps this child is her brother, perhaps her cousin. It doesn't matter.

Cinched high around her tiny waist is a piece of twine. A gourd, split in half, is attached to the twine by a thong.

She ignores the crowd of boys and walks past us, away from us, down along the bank. Her bare feet sink into the mud. The child she is carrying is asleep, his head sideways between her shoulder blades.

The boys are pulling at me, grabbing my arms to get my attention.

She wades into the river, the basin solid upon her head as if it were permanently connected. The dark water stains her sarong. With each step she sinks deeper. She continues out into the river until the water is above her waist and the child's sleeping feet tap the surface.

Her sarong is floating in folds against her, the gourd resting on the water. She unties the gourd from the twine and begins to scoop up cups of brown river. It is a smooth motion. She dips the gourd, gently raises it above her head out over the lip of the basin, and empties it. She cannot see where she is pouring the water. It is somewhere above her head, only her hand knows where. Nothing moves on her body but one arm. She repeats the motion again and again. It is a very large basin and the gourd is small.

I have to drag two boys out of the boat, one with each hand.

The basin is levitating above the river on her head. She cannot see how full the basin is. She feels it. The weight of it.

The boys are pushing and provoking all around me.

She is done. Her arm stops its swiftsmooth motion. She ties the gourd back onto the twine around her waist. She turns and begins to wade back to shore, walking even more with her neck, the folds of her sarong clinging to her little body. She rises out of the water and her sarong is stained the color of the river.

She sees the boys out of the corner of her eye. Then she sees me. She is walking carefully along the bank through the mud, but she sees me coming toward her.

I am talking to her and pointing to my boat. She is wary and keeps walking, pretending not to see me. She has her task. But she is still a child. I can see she is curious. I know she doesn't comprehend my words but she knows what I am saying. Her eyes give her away and she stops. I turn around and start to return to the boat, looking over my shoulder to see if she is following.

She has not moved. She cannot move. She is gazing at me

140

standing very still with the basin on her head, water dripping down her legs, the child's feet poking out along her waist.

I walk back. Standing beside her I realize how small she is. I can see into her basin. The water is motionless. I grasp the sides of the basin and lift. I can barely move it. She doesn't duck. She waits to see if I can raise the basin off her head. I step backward and the water sloshes and I slip in the mud and the basin tips and water pours out and my face burns and she is laughing. I set the basin down in the mud. Half the water is gone.

She follows me to the boat. I try to take her hand to step across the stones but she lets go. She walks behind me through the crowd of boys. They are shouting. I have betrayed them.

I seat myself in the boat and lift her in on my lap. The child is on her back but I am surprised how light she is. Were it not for the weight of the human she is carrying, I believe she would weigh nothing. She would be so buoyant she would simply float up into the air above the brown river.

The boys are upset and contemptuous but I wrench the paddle from them and push out. They grab the boat and try to stop it and I have to hit their hands with the blade.

We glide backward. She is sitting on my lap and the child is resting against my chest. We slip away from the shore, away from the mob of boys and the noise they are making. I let the current turn us. I hold the paddle high and stroke above her head. She places her hands in front of her on the soft skin of the boat.

Her fingers are spread apart. She is feeling the boat gliding through the water. It is the same water that stained her sarong but now she is in it and protected from it. She feels the water going down the sides of the boat, under the boat.

She lifts her hands and gently drops her arms to either side of the kayak. She touches the water, feels the water moving through her fingers.

I take her far out into the river. The boys on the shore grow tiny and insectlike, but she does not look back.

We make a circle so large it doesn't seem like a circle. A circle so wide and long and open we almost reach the other shore.

On the other shore there are women standing in the water washing clothes and singing. They have spread clothes on the bushes to dry. They wave at us.

When I paddle back, many of the boys have dispersed. They are playing somewhere else. I slide into shore and help her up. She steps into the brown water. The weight of the child is hers again.

I follow her up the bank to the basin. She looks down into it but there is no reflection. I lift the basin onto her head.

She walks back down the bank, wades into the water up to her ribs, unties the thong holding the gourd and begins again, catching the river.

I drag my boat up the bank and sit on a leg of root and wait. The few boys still left ignore me.

My compadres return, their packs heavy with food, but they aren't smiling or even talking.

"You guys look like you've just seen a ghost."

Mike lowers his head. "You have to go in."

Rick and John nod dully.

"Planning to."

They don't want to camp here. We get back in our boats and float past a vast rectangle cut out of the bank. There are the remains of a stone deck and broken steps descending into the stagnant water. Once it was a harbor on the river. Now it is a garbage dump.

We find a campsite downstream. None of them want to come into town with me. We have been in the wilderness for days but they are adamantly uninterested.

I take a trail that cuts back to the abandoned harbor. Passing along the edge I see rats feeding on the rubbish in the water. The trail turns into what was once a cobblestone street. I begin to weave through mud huts. All around are forsaken rectangular buildings, their roofs collapsed and trees growing inside, dark holes where the windows used to be.

In a burned-out doorway are four women pounding millet. Their heavy wooden pestles thump a mortar made from a tree trunk. They act as though they don't see me, but look after me when I have passed. Crouched in the shade against the broken houses are men and boys and dogs, their eyes following me like gunsights.

I walk to the center of town. The skeletons of automobiles lie like dead animals in what was once a small square. A pedestal is still there but the statue is gone. The square also once had a circular flower garden. The outline of bricks still exists.

The two-story colonial buildings surrounding the square are vacant. The shutters hang askew, the doors bashed in, the walls disintegrating. Ruins rising above thatched huts.

A railroad station sits across from the square. French colonial architecture. Vines split the stone walls like wedges. The roof tiles are gone so rain falls straight in, rotting the building from the inside out. A few of the smaller rooms have been homesteaded. I can see the light from fires burning on the floor.

I walk down what was apparently a boulevard. Trees were planted in a row but they are hacked stumps now. There were even streetlamps but only a few are still standing; the others are sheared off like broken bottles. The telephone poles droop with broken lines.

I find one building that still seems occupied. It is a bar. When I go inside, it is dark. There is a man with a red face and thinning blond hair at the counter. He buys me a shot before we have said a word to each other.

He is with some arm of the United Nations. A German who has lost his accent. Worked all over the world. Thailand, Chad, Burkina Faso. Economic development projects. Silkworms, hybrid rice, farming techniques. Thirty years of it.

"But this is the worst." He smiles like an old bulldog.

"What happened here?"

He takes a drink before answering. "They fucked them-selves."

I ask him about the railroad station. He tells me foreign money and foreign contractors built the railroad. They wanted to link Conakry on the coast with Kankan in the interior. They imagined Kouroussa as a thriving river port. A big little African city. Goods moving up and down the Niger—bananas, rice, bolts of cloth, bales of cotton. Cranes shifting cargo from the boats to the train cars and from the train cars into the boats.

"Of course they had to buy off the chiefs."

He orders another round for both of us.

"Even today it's twenty percent of every contract in Africa. Fucking millions of dollars. You know what the chiefs do with the money? They buy fleets of Mercedeses and send their children to school in England. Of course the bloody children never come back."

He rubs his burnt face.

"The railroad was years ago, but then it was the same with the communications system. They wanted telephones so we paid off the chiefs and got them telephones."

"What went wrong?"

"Nothing! It was the same old thing. When the contracts ended, the telephones stopped working."

"Weren't people trained to fix them?"

"Of course. But the chiefs wouldn't allow it. They wanted more money. They wouldn't let their people fix the phones unless we gave them more money. Their Mercedeses were breaking down. But there was no more money."

Sweat is dripping off his face. He wipes his forehead with the back of his arm.

"And now it's all gone to hell, as you have so keenly noticed. Every bit of it kaput. The railroad, the phones, even the fucking highway is disappearing back into the bush.

"Once they had medicine; now they have no medicine.

Once they had work; now there is no work. For God's sake!" He is almost weeping. "Once their children were well fed; now their children are hungry!"

I am watching some children in the street through a broken window. They are playing with a length of wire, hitting each other.

"Africa's fucked. It fucked itself."

I finish my drink. He stares at the floor.

"Asia is better. People work in Asia. Africans . . . *Africans!* All they do is fuck off."

"So why—"

"Hope!" His voice croaks. "*Mein Gott*, what else! It's all we have."

I start to respond but he cuts me off again.

"I know!" He is shouting. "I know, I know, I know. I'm a fool."

He puts his head back, downs his drink, and tips his shot glass at me.

"No thanks."

"Suit yourself."

The barman pours him another drink.

Instead of returning to camp I follow the railroad tracks toward the river. The rails are still there, grass two feet high between them. Most of the ties are rotten. They were not properly coated with creosote. Many of the spikes have been pried out.

I go out onto the bridge. It was once a railroad bridge, connecting white people with black people. The railroad is gone now and there are no white people left. The bridge has become a footbridge. The villagers no longer have to take dugouts across the river.

I walk to the middle of the bridge and lean through the rusted girders and look at the water. It is as dark as dirt. I can't see down inside it. I can see only the surface.

It is dusk when I leave the bridge. Weaving through the

thatched huts I hear hammering and follow the sound to the remnants of a building hidden deep in the trees.

A man squats beside a crude oven. The oven has been built from the bricks of the building. The man notices me but moves his eyes back to the coals. Beside him a little boy covered with charcoal dust is jumping up and down on a skin bag. It is a bellows. The coals glow red with each pounce. Two railroad spikes lie in the coals, orange from the heat.

The blacksmith pulls out the spikes with his tongs and drops them on a makeshift anvil. Squatting in the dirt, hammer in one hand and tongs in the other, he pounds the two spikes together, smashing them into one. They chip and spark. After several hits he flips the lump over and continues pounding until the metal has grown gray and inflexible. Then he lifts the lump with his tongs and puts it back in the coals and the little boy starts working the bellows again and the blacksmith wipes the sweat from his face.

I don't have to ask him what he is forging. Lying in the dirt beside him, already fastened to a stick, is the blade of a hoe.

Back at camp we argue into the night. We each have our own opinion but John and I aren't talking much. We don't have to. Rick and Mike will cover all the bases.

Rick maintains that Kouroussa is just more proof of the injustice of white imperialism, the unavoidable result of exploitation and avarice. He is more convinced than ever that wherever whites go they destroy the culture.

Mike argues that the quality of life for the villagers would have been better if the railroad and the telephones were still working. He sets up a scenario: A father, seriously ill, with nine children, needs medical attention. With the railroad the man could go to a hospital in Conakry. With a phone he could call for help. Either way he might live instead of die and thus continue to work and support his family.

Rick disagrees. He suggests that the man might not be allowed to use the railroad or the telephone. The whites might not let him.

"Bullshit!" says Mike. "Blacks use railroads and telephones everywhere in Africa."

Rick is not sure he likes this idea. He suggests that telephones and railroads are inappropriate technologies designed by whites to manipulate blacks. Capitalist tools used to seduce Africans into adopting Western ideals.

And medicine? Education?

Rick mounts a reasoned argument that even medicine is not necessarily good. Especially Western medicine. It can prolong life when it should not be prolonged. He thinks it's too bad we don't have saber-toothed tigers anymore.

"Saber-toothed tigers didn't just take the old and infirm," says Mike. "They killed babies and children."

"So you say," replies Rick.

"Lose somebody you love; then let's talk."

"I have."

Rick moves on to education. He thinks village education, whatever it may be, is certainly better than anything formal and foreign. He thinks the American system of education is a joke. We should go back to apprenticeship. "Grade school is fine, everybody has to learn their three Rs, but after that each child should be put with a master craftsman and taught a trade."

"Absurd," says Mike. "I wish the world were so simple! What about biologists, engineers, physicists, surgeons? What about theory?"

Rick says theory is what gets us into trouble.

"Theory is just a tool," says Mike. "Calculus is to an engineer what a level is to a carpenter."

The debate goes on like a volleyball game. Some nice serves, some bobbles, some irretrievable spikes.

Rick convinces us he is a Luddite. The argument comes full circle and he states again that village education is just fine for their world.

"Their world is our world," says Mike.

"That's what we made it."

"No. That's what it is."

We leave first thing in the morning and the discussion inevitably starts up again. Rick and Mike debating as we paddle out onto the fulvous sea. They are both educated and intelligent and stubborn and right, so I am listening, but not really. I slide into an eddy for one last look back.

There is a little girl up high on the red bridge above the brown water. She has stuck her hand between the girders; a basin is on her head so she cannot lean out. I don't know if it is the child from yesterday. She is too far away. She could be that girl, she could be any girl. She is waving at us.

Back when we were searching for a put-in, near the village of Mamouria, Sori took me to the hut of a distinguished chief. I had a question and he said this chief was very wise and could answer it.

Sori went into the hut first. He was inside several minutes before stepping out. He said I could go in now; he would wait outside. I ducked my head and entered, exchanging blazing light for penumbral shade.

"Welcome."

The chief was very old and very tall. He stooped like all men who are that tall. He was in a tattered hide skirt. His skin sagged around his knees and elbows.

He was folding an envelope and placing it on a shelf pegged into the wall. He said it was his military disability check from France. The check would be carried by foot to a bank in a small town, cashed, then the money passed back through the jungle. It was a small amount. It helped support his village.

The French had conscripted him in 1940. He was in the Free French forces and fought the Italians at the Kufra Oases. Then he was put on a ship to England. The ship was blown apart by the Germans near Malta. Only he and seven other men survived. They were picked out of the ocean by a Spanish gunship. Afterward, after he lived through the operations, he was sent to a hospital in England to learn how to walk again. He stayed in England for nine years. That is where he learned English.

When he returned to his village, he was an important man. He went away a rickety tall boy with knobby dry knees and came back with scars and money.

"But that is not what you wanted to talk about."

"No."

"You wish to know why our women are cut."

"I do."

"That is simple. Because if they were not, one man could never satisfy a woman. A woman would need many men."

"I don't believe that."

He laughed. "Yes, of course. You could not."

I wasn't sure whether he was insulting me.

"Well then, I shall just say it is our custom."

"It is a barbaric custom."

"Please"—a sneer passed briefly across his face—"do not speak to me of barbarism."

"Are your own wives *cut*?"

"It is not possible for a woman to marry if she has not been circumcised."

"It is not circumcision. It is castration."

He sighed.

"But why? You have seen the outside world."

"Yes, I have."

"And it is still done here, in your village?"

"Yes."

"To all of them?"

"Yes, at age seven."

He was not offended. I could ask him anything.

"How is it done?"

"It used to be done with a knife. A small knife, very sharp. Now it is sometimes done with a razor blade."

"Who does it?"

"The old women of the village."

"They hold them down."

"I have not seen it."

But I was seeing it. A little girl screaming and convulsing with fear and they sit on her arms and spread her legs and sit on her little knees and her stomach is quivering and they spread her labium and begin cutting and the blood is warm flowing off her into the dirt and the little girl's mouth is open and her eyes brilliant from the horror because she believes she is dying.

"It will not continue."

"Perhaps."

"It is unspeakable."

"Yes, we do not speak of it."

"It should be spoken of. Everyone should talk about it."

"There would be problems."

"There should be problems."

He smiled wearily.

On the trail gliding through the high grass where long ago we could have been killed by a lion but now there are none, I had asked Sori if he believed in this practice.

"Iss not in Koran."

"Then you do not do it."

"No."

"Then your daughters cannot be married?"

"They marry."

"Sori, what if it were in the Koran."

"Then I do it."

And we had kept on quietly and easily through the high grass where once there were lions.

The chief seated himself on a low stool, slowly leaned his back against the mud wall, and crossed his legs under his skirt.

"May I tell you something?"

"All right."

"Do you know what all white people fear most?"

"I do not know all white people."

"White people fear the fear of pain."

"And black people don't?"

"Yes. But it is not the same. We believe pain is necessary. We accept it. It is part of life. We even celebrate it."

"Nonsense. You live with it."

"Yes. Yes exactly. We don't run from it."

"You misjudge me. It is not just the pain; it is the loss."

"Ah, but it is a gain. Freedom from desire."

"And men do not require such freedom?"

"A man without desire is not a man."

"And a woman?"

"She is a wife and a mother. A better wife. A better mother."

"I do not believe this."

"Yes, of course."

He offered me the stool beside him and began to clean his fingernails with a stick.

"When I was in England, I learned many things. I was a boarder at Mrs. Rollins's residence on Chatfield Road. She was very kind to me. She called me Meto because she could not pronounce my name. Many times she said to me, "'Never mind, Meto, underneath we are all the same.'"

He paused for my reaction. I had none.

"Do you know what I think? I think Mrs. Rollins needed to believe this. I think all white people need to believe this. I don't know why. It is not true. We are not the same."

"I believe we are."

"Yes, of course. But you do see then?"

"No. See what?"

He clasped his hands and took a long breath through his nose. He was waiting. Allowing me time to think about what he had said.

"Do you know what your guide Sori Keita told me?"

I shook my head.

"He said you could walk like a Malinke. That is why I agreed to speak with you. He said you could walk like we black men walk, that inside, you were a black man. This concerned me very much. But now I have spoken with you and I am relieved. You are white. Inside and out."

He raised his hand, cutting me off.

151

"I know. You don't believe this."

"I don't."

"Now you must see?"

"I don't."

The chief wore an expression of complacent exaspera-
tion.

"We, you and I, we don't believe in the same things. How
could we possibly be the same?"

Sori's head came into the hut below the beam.

"We must go now."

I stood up. The chief stood up. I shook his hand.

"Thank you for the conversation."

"Not at all. Farewell, white man."

When we pass the mouth of the Niandan, another tributary
with its source deep in the Fouta Djallon, our river swells to
twice its previous width. The Niger is now a half mile wide.

We begin to spot the occasional pirogue. We have seen
dugouts carrying people bank to bank, but pirogues are
transport vessels, the gondolas of the Niger. Shaped like a
swordfish, with a long pointed prow well above the water
and a squared-off stern fin, laden with a cargo of oranges or
bananas or reed mats, they are poled through the water.
One man is balanced out on the prow, the other on the stern
plank. These men wave only if we wave at them, and sometimes not then. Their work is arduous and tedious beyond
belief. Perhaps waving would break their trance.

The boats are a welcome sight and a disappointment. The
Niger is no longer ours. Rick and John become voluble, as if
their anchors had been chopped away and they were set
free.

Mike has become sullen. Well before Kouroussa, as soon
as the life went out of the river, he began slipping inside
himself. He would prop the shortwave up on his bow and
listen for hours, paddling miles behind us as if he were
drugged. Now the radio is strapped permanently to his

deck. The river has become so limp there is nothing that could throw it off. He bought twenty pounds of batteries in Kouroussa and listens constantly to the BBC. An hour of Ukrainian folk songs. And now, the news. A crisp outline, a coup somewhere, a leader abdicates, a people revolt—then the stories in detail, then recap. An hour of debate about the crisis in Nigeria or Sierra Leone or Chad. Cricket scores. And now, the news.

Day by day, one bite at a time, the emptiness of the river is devouring Michael.

It is also eating me.

I paddle alone along the bank searching for animals. But there are no animals anymore. Perhaps in some isolated locations a few hippos and crocs still exist, but they are hiding out, taking their revenge on the innocent or the unlucky. We have left the wilderness and reentered civilization. Wherever there are people, the animals have been killed. It has always been this way.

I try to play games in my head with the clouds or the waves but it doesn't help. Games only make you crazier. The mind is too quick. You can think through too much in just a minute, and out here in this vacuum of space minutes are hours and hours weeks and weeks years.

As the days pass, I begin to feel numb, vaguely deranged. To combat my psychosis I do what I have always done in times of ceaseless, senseless boredom; I leave. Abscond. Most of the time I leap into the future and spend hours with Sue living our life together having our baby, but then when I have to come back the sadness is like g-forces on my heart. So the next time I slip back to the books I have read and reread, whole sections verbatim.

North Africa and West Africa and much of the Sahara were once rich with wildlife. At the time of Christ vast herds of elephants still roamed the veld. These were the elephants Alexander the Great had used to conquer Persia. The Greeks taught the Carthaginians to catch them and train them. But the elephants trampled crops and the farmers began to kill them. And the cartilage of the elephant's trunk

153

became a Roman delicacy. And ivory became a Roman adornment, fashioned into grotesquely heavy bracelets and necklaces. And in this way all the elephants were slaughtered.

And gazelles and hartebeests and wildebeests and zebras and leopards and lions. Once they were all here and the Sahel was not a wasteland. But the fleet-footed were speared to make room for herds of sheep and cattle, and the lions were trapped and shipped back to Rome for the spectacles of carnage.

Caesar put 400 lions with 400 gladiators into the arena. Let the true predators be victorious. The nobles of Pompeii one-upped him, pitting 600 lions against 600 gladiators. Augustus held twenty-six such celebrations of murder during his reign, butchering 3,500 lions. For the grand opening of the Colosseum in the first century, Titus provided 9,000 lions to kill or be killed by 9,000 gladiators. Some years later, Trajan had 2,246 lions slain in a single day. . . .

But then the bloodbath is too great and I wing back to the present and look down on myself like a bird or an angel and find I am still where I was before I left, on a liquid brown highway a hundred lanes wide.

From high above I bank wide and make a U-turn, this time paging back through my own life as if it were a novel I liked but didn't always understand.

We traveled east along the coastline of Algeria, often walking, sleeping under bridges or in orchard shacks or rolled up in our jackets on the beach. We were walking the road when we reached the border between Algeria and Tunisia.

The officer at the Algerian check post smiled at us through his mustache. We thought he would ask for our passports but he didn't. He guided us into a small room. Three other soldiers came in behind him and closed the door. The officer asked us where our luggage was. We told him we had been robbed. He nodded and asked us to strip.

What?

He nodded again. We handed him our passports. He looked at them, passed them back, and told us to strip. We refused. He noticed I was fingering something in my pocket and told me to hand it over. I did. It was a compass. The thieves had dropped it and we had found it in the thorn bushes in the morning.

The officer started playing with the compass. Without looking up, he told us to take off our jackets. As we did this, the soldiers standing behind him started whistling, catcalling. The officer didn't pay any attention. He was captivated by the compass, rotating it in his hand and watching the needle return again and again. He apparently didn't know it was a tool for navigation; he thought it was a toy. One of the soldiers checked the pockets of our jackets and then motioned for us to take off our pants. We shook our heads. The eyes of the soldier shot back to the officer. He was still playing with the compass. The other two soldiers stepped forward. They had undone their belts and opened their pants.

Suddenly the officer popped the compass in the air with his thumb, caught it, slipped it into his shirt pocket, and said something to the soldiers. They protested but he just waved his hand. One of them reluctantly closed up his pants and opened the door and we ran out.

In the no-man's-land between the two countries there was a mountain. We walked along the windy road hoping to hitch a ride but no vehicles passed by. On the other side of the mountain the road began to zigzag down through the trees. We could see the curves below us and decided to save time by cutting straight down. Somehow we lost the road and didn't find it again until dark. We knew we had missed the Tunisian border station but we weren't about to go back.

From out of nowhere a taxi appeared. It stopped alongside us in the dark and a door swung open. We never took taxis. We hardly ever even took buses. Mike leaned into the cab and told the driver we didn't need a ride, but the driver insisted. He spoke little English but apparently he was on his way home and would give us a ride for free.

I got in the front seat and Mike crawled into the back. For some reason the driver drove with the ceiling light on. We tried to make small talk but it petered out. Mike and I started getting drowsy. When I looked over my shoulder, Mike's head had slid against the window. I slouched and leaned against the car door.

My eyes were drooping when I started feeling uneasy. I glanced over at the driver.

"*Mike!*"

The driver was gaping at me, his tongue hanging out. He had his pants down around his ankles and his ass up off the seat and was steering with his knees and jerking off with both hands.

Mike came up from behind and cracked him so hard on the side of the head we started swerving and the driver's feet were tangled in his pants and we were all over the road and he was coming all over the dashboard and he finally slammed on the brakes and Mike and I rolled out.

We reached Tunis several days later. We had told ourselves that at Tunis we would start south again for Timbuktu, but we didn't. We hung out in the French quarter ogling the girls. They were gorgeous. We were unwashed infidels and they were smooth-skinned French/Arabic females. They didn't even wear veils. We talked about their dark eyes and their hidden tits. That's when we started thinking about Europe again, how much fun it had been. How in Europe we could eat pizza and regale girls who understood English with our stories of Africa. Compared with this, going to Timbuktu, probably just some mud village in the desert anyway, seemed ridiculous.

We weren't really explorers and we knew it. We were travelers, adventurers, misadventurers at our best. We didn't have the intensely noble, blindly vain zeal of a true explorer.

We didn't have the indefatigable perseverance or the imperial mission. We were never really searching for anything more than ourselves.

Our cockroach room was right on the docks. We spent several days trying to find a ship that would let us work for passage. The blackamoor corsairs stared at us the way the border soldiers had and the ship captains refused even to talk with us. Eventually we decided just to fork over the cash and take the ferry.

When we passed through customs, the officer confiscated our passports and motioned us out of line. We waited while everyone else boarded the ship. Then the officer led us into a small room. He shut the door and asked us where we had come from. We said Algeria. He frowned. We had no exit stamp in our passport from Algeria. We also had no entrance stamp for Tunisia. That made us illegal aliens. He was sorry, but he would have to take us to jail.

We claimed ignorance. We said we had stopped at the border station but the soldiers must have forgotten to stamp our passports. That wasn't our fault! How could that be our fault.

He said we would not like jail here in Tunisia, in Africa. It wasn't like jail in America. Young men like us, well . . . He made an obscene gesture with his fingers.

All we wanted to do was go back to Europe. We again protested our innocence but he knew we were lying and we were too frightened to know all he wanted was money. He rubbed his thumb over his fingers several times before we got the hint. We each had to pay him twenty dollars. He slipped the money in his shirt pocket, led us out of the room, briskly stamped our passports, and wished us a pleasant voyage.

Then I blink and the present reappears: a desert of brown water. No matter where I go I am still on a river wider than a lake, longer than an ocean.

When we were first planning this trip, I thought boating all day every day for days would be like being on a long bike tour. I figured paddling would resemble pedaling. But I was wrong. I should have known. On a bicycle you pass directly through the landscape. This is not possible in a kayak. In a kayak you can see only the banks. You are so low in the water you cannot see above them or beyond them. They confine you. You are not traveling through the landscape, you are traveling alongside it, forever curious, forever wondering, forever yearning to know what the world is like beyond the banks.

The river is so immense now it has large islands inside it. We never know which side to choose, but it doesn't make any difference. Sometimes there are still crosscurrents. The only ones you can readily identify are the eddylines near the bank. But even out in the middle of the river they are there; you just can't see them. The surface is flat but your boat is suddenly being pulled one way or another. It has to do with what is underneath the river. The bedrock. You never know what it looks like; you can only guess from the behavior of the water.

Crosscurrents are the only thing that remind us of where we are, like when you're inside a plane and it jumps and the fasten seatbelt light springs on. We are passing over Africa at thirty thousand feet. Nothing to see out the windows, so naturally we're living in our heads.

I didn't come to Africa to be in my head. Nor did Mike. But I sense it is different for Rick and John.

Rick seems quite comfortable, as if the Niger were an immense sofa for him. He looks forward to the thousands of free hours. When I ask him how it's going, he says he's getting into the Zen of it.

John specifically said he needed time to think—what better place than all by yourself on an ocean. Just you and endless miles of flatwater. When I ask him how it's going, he says he's listening to the river.

When I ask Mike how it's going, he says okay. This is not a Mike answer. He cannot live with okay. He came to Africa solely for the adventure and now that the adventure is over, he has left.

I can't stay either. I try. I try to listen to the river and get into the Zen of paddling and it works for a few days, but it's like fasting. I think I'm doing it, think I could do it forever, gradually becoming thinner and thinner until I just vanished, when suddenly my mind intrudes and says this is horseshit and I need to eat.

While Clapperton was searching for the Niger's mouth in the interior, another Scotsman, Major Alexander Gordon Laing, had been leading expeditions into the Fouta Djallon in search of the Niger's source. Major Laing came within fifty miles before he was turned back by hostile tribes. By then Clapperton and Denham had returned with their mission unfulfilled. Laing had seized the opportunity and successfully lobbied the British government to become its next African explorer.

Because he knew the region, Laing wanted to start from the west coast. But Clapperton and Denham had proven the northern route, and he was forced to start from Tripoli. He spent several months in North Africa preparing, abruptly married the daughter of the British consul on 14 July 1825, then struck out into the desert, the marriage unconsummated.

Laing was intent on taking a direct route south through the Sahara. This had not been attempted since the time of the Romans. He had three men with him, a manservant named Jack le Bore and two shipwrights. The team was called the Timbuktu Mission.

But Clapperton was right on Laing's heels, having spent less than three months back home with his family before setting off for Africa again. He would soon be arriving at the Gulf of Guinea and would progress north from there with a large party that included his manservant Richard Lander and a Captain Pearce.

Earlier that year the Geographical Society of Paris had put up a 10,000-franc reward for the first man to reach Timbuktu and return to Europe alive. The two men knew of each other. Hence, it was a race.

Laing rode camels south through the blazing desert; Clapperton paddled north up the Lagos River. By 1826 both men were eight hundred miles from Timbuktu. Clapperton had penetrated deep into Yoruba country, several of his men including Pearce having already died of malaria. Laing was in the sands owned by the Tuaregs.

Meanwhile, the French had mounted their own expedition. A man named Beaufort was to start from the west coast. He was well financed. He died shortly after arriving.

Then an archaeologist, Giovanni Battista Belzoni, set out for Timbuktu by himself from the southern coast. A giant, flamboyant Italian, Belzoni had begun his career as a circus strongman and later became famous for opening the pyramids of Egypt. He made it ten miles before contracting dysentery and dying.

Laing and Clapperton, both accompanied by their faithful menservants, were pushing onward. Clapperton and Lander battling delirium and fever in the jungle, Laing and le Bore the horrific hardships of desert travel.

Clapperton reached the Niger at Busa, the place where Mungo Park was said to have been ambushed. He was the first to find evidence of the tragedy. After interviewing several natives, he continued upriver.

Laing was still in the Sahara. A band of heavily armed Tuaregs joined his caravan. Six days later, just before dawn, the Tuaregs attacked Laing while he was asleep. They shot into his tent, then plunged in slashing and hacking with swords. Once he was murdered, they eviscerated one of the shipwrights, slaughtered several others, and packed off into the black desert.

But Laing was not dead:

To begin from the top: I have five sabre cuts on the crown of the head and three on the left temple, all fractures from which much bone has come away, one on my left cheek which fractured the jaw bone and has divided the ear, forming a very unsightly wound; one over the right temple and a dreadful gash on the back of the neck, which slightly scratched the windpipe; a musket ball in the hip, which made its way through my back, slightly grazing the backbone; five sabre cuts on my right arm and hand, three of the fingers broken, the hand cut three-fourths across, and the wrist bones cut through; three cuts on the left arm, the bone of which has been broken but is again uniting; one slight wound on the right leg and two with one dreadful gash on the left.

In three weeks Major Gordon Laing felt he was sufficiently healed to ride a camel. He *would* reach Timbuktu. The next village they passed through was consumed with a plague. His manservant Jack le Bore and his other shipwright died. Laing was sick for nine days.

Clapperton was still struggling north along the Niger. At the city of Sokoto he left his manservant Richard Lander to guard their meager belongings and carried on alone.

On 13 August 1826, Major Gordon Laing, crippled and disfigured, rode into Timbuktu. He had been in the desert for over one year and had traveled 2,650 miles. If he was shocked by what he saw, he didn't let on. He claimed Timbuktu was all that he expected.

Timbuktu was, however, in a state of anarchy and Laing's life was in constant danger. He was urged by the sultan to leave as soon as possible, which he did. Thirty miles north of Timbuktu, on the second day of his journey home, he was again attacked. This time he was beheaded.

Clapperton was duped and stymied by rapacious chiefs and rejoined Lander. Tribes were warring all around them. Clapperton was again laid low by malaria and dysentery. His condition grew worse month after month and he died, cradled in Lander's arms, on 13 April 1827.

Lander attempted to take up where Clapperton left off,

but he too was frustrated by war. Half a year later he made his way back to the Gulf of Guinea. En route he was given a shirt of Thomas Park's, son of Mungo, who had set out to determine the circumstances of his father's death but died instead. On the coast Lander was captured by cannibals and made to drink poison. They intended to eat his heart but he escaped, forced himself to vomit, and survived to return to England.

One afternoon Mike starts shooting. We are pulling into an island for lunch and he lifts his pistol, holds it steady, and begins firing at a dead tree. Scares the daylights out of Rick and John.

That evening, when the light is a dusty pink, Mike glides up beside me. His radio is not on. For a while we don't talk. We paddle in synchronization, drops of water flying into the air like sparks.

"I can't stop thinking about Diana."

"I know."

"I keep wondering how she's doing. How they're doing."

"I know."

"Do you think about Sue?"

"All the time. I try not to."

"Don't you feel guilty?"

"They're tough. They're fine. They're happy to have some time of their own before it's gone forever."

"You're rationalizing."

"I am."

"You're talking about you."

We are stroking close enough that sometimes we nick paddles. An hour quietly passes.

"Mark."

"Mike."

"It's getting damn hard to justify."

"I know."

We go along together for another hour. It is dusk; the sky violet. The day is almost over.

"Buck, the thrill is gone."

"Yes, it is."

"If I'm going to spend the whole day thinking about her, I might as well be with her."

We are no longer parallel so our boats begin to drift apart. He looks over at me. It is unusual to see sorrow in Mike's face.

"I just keep thinking . . . I just keep thinking about all the things Diana and I could be doing together."

The river is now over a mile wide and entirely navigable. We have seen pirogues and punts and barges. For me and Mike, it is no longer a river for kayaks. At the next town, Siguiri, there is regular ferry service to all the large cities downriver—Bamako, Ségou, Djenné. We don't even discuss it. At Siguiri, Mike and I will leave the Niger.

That night, camped on a sandbar in the middle of the river, Mike tells Rick and John.

They are outraged, so upset they can hardly speak.

"The headwaters are over, guys. We did it."

"We didn't come here just to do the headwaters!"

John and Rick feel betrayed. They say they can't believe we are abandoning them. Mike glances at me.

Mike and I have children due in two months. Rick and John have unlimited amounts of time. No reason to go home, no one to go home to.

We try to talk it out but they are too hurt. They say we can do what we want but they are staying on the river. To them it is immoral to quit. For us it is immoral to continue.

A RIDE

At Siguiri the riverbank is bedlam. Motorized punts with humans packed in like cattle, canopied pirogues sinking under their cargo of vegetables or fruit, foul-smelling fishing dhows, prehistoric dugouts.

Lined up in the mud along the bank are a dozen rickshaws loaded with plastic jugs. Between the scows drooling rainbows of fuel and the women sudsing clothes, athletic young boys are filling the five-gallon jugs. Once they are full, they will push the carts into town and make their deliveries of drinking water. It makes me think of Archimedes.

Two thousand years ago in Egypt, Archimedes was standing on the banks of the Nile watching boys fill clay jugs. At some point he seated himself and with pen and papyrus invented a simple spiral tube that could raise water up out of the river and run it down an aqueduct into the city.

But we are fortunate the waterboys are here. Carting the boats of four pink men pays better than hauling water. They load our kayaks onto their rickshaws and trot them into town like floats in a parade, depositing them outside a mud building they claim is a hotel.

We step inside and look around. It is dark and reeks of beer. There are half a dozen small doors off a barroom. Two slackboned women in worn slips lean against the bar. They turn their heads lazily to look at us.

Back outside, Rick and John are morose and stand in the shade while Mike and I help each other dismantle our boats.

We are taxidermists in reverse. I unwrap the splints holding my vessel together and it collapses like the skin of an animal with the skeleton removed. Just as in the beginning, we are surrounded by an inquisitive crowd. I give away the broken ribs of my boat and the kids dance around holding them in the air like trophies. In less than an hour our ships are back inside duffel bags.

The proprietor offers us our pick of the cavelike rooms, each with its own carnal history, swaybacked bed and stained sheets. They are a couple of bucks each. For a couple more you can have a guest. His eyes don't twinkle. We put our tents up in the backyard.

There is the team gear to divvy up. Medical kit, boat repair kit, field kitchen, books, maps, spare kayak equipment, the letters Mike and I obtained from the embassies. We give all of it to Rick and John. They will need it. They will have to make the decisions now. We offer them the guns but they shake their heads resolutely.

That night we get good and drunk together. Alcohol is a blessing. Suddenly we enjoy each other's company again, re-remember we are friends. We reminisce about our adventure, boast and laugh.

When we stumble to our separate tents, Mike falls asleep instantly. He went home days ago. Now it is only a matter of his body catching up.

I lie awake and listen to him breathe. I can hear movement in one of the rooms. I can hear Rick and John. I can't make out what they are saying but they are talking and talking. I gaze up at the stars through the netting of the tent.

Later everything grows quiet. I am still awake. I unzip the screen, crawl out, zip it up, and walk through the moonlight into the whorehouse. The barroom is dim, tenebrous. Mosquitoes are bobbing around the light on the ceiling. One of the two women we saw when we first arrived is asleep at a table, her head between her arms. I go behind the bar, get myself a bottle of warm beer, open it, and sit down in a chair along the wall.

When she wakes up, she lifts her head, blinks, sees me. I

am not inclined to speak, I just nod. She drops her head back into the cradle of her arms, then looks up again.

She comes over to me. She is barefoot, her legs thin and bowed. Her slip is ratty and soiled. She drags up a chair and sits down close beside me. I go over to the bar, get a glass, empty the rest of my beer into it, and hand it to her. She smiles but doesn't take a drink. She rests the glass on her knee.

Her cheekbones protrude and she has black rings under her eyes. She is frail, almost ghastly. Her skin is leprous. I don't know what disease she has, but she is dying from it, and she knows it.

We sit together without speaking. After a while she leans against me.

I think I must make a decision.

Mike is going home. Home to Diana and their unborn child inside her. Rick and John will keep boating. When they return home, they will admit that they hated it. Rick will confess that he grew to despise the dirt villages along the river. All the balloonbellied, sticklegged, grimyfingered children screaming "*Cadeaux, cadeaux, cadeaux.*" I suspect that Rick and John are kayaking the Niger just so they can say they did it. I have done this before. Sometimes it is a good enough reason; sometimes it isn't. Back in Wyoming they will give lectures at Rotary Clubs saying they did the river and we didn't.

But this always happens. All four of us will remember a completely different trip, almost as though we were never together at all. Every journey is unfathomably personal. When it is over, you always see yourself as someone different from who you were during the journey, because you are.

But what am I doing? Going home to Sue? I think I must make a decision.

The woman and I have sat together for a long time before I recognize my own concealment. It is like something you put in a hiding place for safekeeping and then forget about and believe you have lost forever, only to discover it months or even years later right where you left it. I made the decision a long time ago. I am going to Timbuktu.

167

She has not taken a drink from the glass. She has simply sat there in the chair beside me, leaning lightly against me, staring at the floor.

As I start to get up, she takes my hand and looks up. She pulls me toward her and kisses my forehead.

My eyes split open like tiny black seeds. The tilting and sliding slowed, then stopped. I was staring sideways at a wall.

I didn't know where I was. The air seemed miasmal, gluey. My eyes raced across the room. I didn't recognize a thing. I was completely disoriented. I sat up and swung my legs to the floor.

There was a man lying on a bunk in the corner in the dark. I stared at him. His hair was in his face, one leg uncovered. I could hear him breathing.

Mike?

It all rushed back instantly. I was in Africa. We were in Tunis. In the morning we would sail to Europe.

My journal was lying on the floor. For a moment I thought I should write down how strange it felt to not know where you were or even who you were, but then I thought why? What was the point? The idea of keeping a journal suddenly seemed ridiculous. All those pages and pages of idiotic scrawl. Why couldn't I just let it all happen to me. I didn't have to document it. If I didn't remember it later, so what? It was my life.

I looked at my watch. Fifteen till three. I should lie down and go back to sleep. *Why?* I'm not tired! There isn't anyone telling me what to do anymore. I am a man. I stood up and got dressed.

The smell of the sea was in the street. It woke me up and I realized I needed to piss. I stopped in the middle of the street and pulled down my pants and pulled it out and went. I knew I was letting perversity sprout inside me, but for once I didn't care.

I walked down to the dock and stared into the water. It

was motionless and greasy. I stared up at the ships. They sat in the water heavier than the buildings sat on the street. Their hulls were scabrous, so rotted and festered it was as if they were just waiting for the paint to peel off.

On a corner there was a bar, a sailors' bar. The lights were on so I went in. There was a man sitting in a chair with his arms crossed and his eyes closed. He had tattoos on his forearms. When I came in, he stood up and walked around the bar. I went to a stool and sat down.

I wasn't thirsty but I ordered a beer. I wasn't hungry either but I ordered a sandwich. The bartender sliced open the bread with a large knife and dug out a trough and dropped in two cold fried eggs, put the sandwich on a plate, and pushed it in front of me.

I drank the beer and ate the sandwich, then ordered another beer. I was trying to act like this was all normal stuff for me. Hanging out in a dangerous part of an African port in the dead of night.

When she showed up, she was leaning against the lamppost in the street. I let my eyes settle on her. I was going to look away after a minute but I didn't. I was a stranger in a strange land. No one knew me. I knew no one. I could do anything I damn well pleased.

The pole was behind her back and her head was down. I couldn't see her face. She was holding the pole with her hands, her shoulders and her ass against the pole, her breasts pointing out.

I let myself stare at her body, greedily, as if her body were all she was. As if she were headless. I let myself think about the things I only dreamed about. The kinds of things you believed could never happen with any of the girls you knew.

I was imagining what was under her dress, what she looked like naked, when, without looking up, as if summoned, she pushed away from the lamppost, walked into the bar and came directly toward me.

Somehow I had thought I was safe staring through the window, but she came up behind me and pressed the front of her body against my back and the muscles in my legs began to quiver.

Something was on my thighs. I looked down between my legs. Her hands. She was passing her fingertips along the insides of my thighs. I could have stopped her right then, but I didn't.

I was trying to get up the courage to turn around. When I finally did, I thought she would hang on to me but she just let go, as if she knew the moment I would move.

All I needed to do was walk past her. Just step off the stool and put one foot in front of the other and walk out. Go back to our room, back to bed, wake up with Mike and leave for Europe like a decent young man from Wyoming. And that's what part of me wanted to do. But I couldn't. This was why I had come out. This was what I had secretly hoped would happen.

She passed out the door and crossed through the green pool of light beneath the lamppost and suffused into the darkness and I followed her. She walked one block, stopped, turned so I could see her figure in profile, then disappeared into a doorway.

When I got there, the door was open. I found her inside in the dark. The darkness reassured me. I pulled her toward me and started pawing her, trying to pull her dress up.

Suddenly there was a flash of lurid yellow light. We were inside a bunker. Stained concrete walls, an iron bed, a filthy mattress. I pulled the string hanging from the bulb.

Again a vomitous yellow light splattered the room. She was holding out her hand. I was trying not to but I was shaking. I started to put my hand in hers but she slapped it away and stuck her hand out again. I fumbled in my pants under my shirt and tore open my money belt and pulled out a bill. She ripped it from my hand and slugged me.

My hands were not working properly and I finally jerked out more money and she snatched it out of my hand. Then she started sliding down unbuttoning my pants and I was against her trying to pull her dress over her head but she wouldn't let me. She was kneeling and I couldn't move and

I tried to lift her and she thrust her head down and tightened her mouth but that wasn't what I wanted. I wanted to see her body. I wanted her to take off her dress. I tried to lift her off me and she bit hard and I groaned. Then she stood up. She stared at me with a smile I had never seen in my life, and then slowly pulled her dress over her head. She stopped with the folds concealing her face and the horrid yellow light was upon her body and I saw the round dark burns on her nipples and all over her breasts and the wide swollen scars that were never stitched slashing up her stomach like on a gutted fish and everything started to collapse.

In the morning Rick and John approach our tent. They say they have talked it over. They have changed their minds. They want one of the guns and all the ammo. I give them mine.

Before noon a Toyota minivan pulls up outside the whorehouse. The driver heard there were two white guys, *toobobs*, who wanted a ride to Bamako. The minivan is so battered it looks as if it had been hit by an elephant. The roof rack is a mountain of boxes and vinyl suitcases. There are arms and heads hanging out all the windows. Mike and I count twenty-one people inside. The driver looks at us and laughs.

His assistant agilely swings himself atop the mountain of luggage. Rick and John help us hand up our boat bags and our packs and the assistant ties them on; but he does a half-assed job so Mike clambers on top and tightens the ropes while the people inside crane their heads out the windows trying to see what the crazy toobob is doing.

We already asked how much a ticket costs but when we pay, the driver becomes indignant. He doesn't speak English but he makes it clear we should pay double. Mike and I know it is because we are white. We won't stand for it. We've been in Africa before. We start yelling at him and he starts yelling at us.

A very tall black man squeezes out of the minivan. He wears a flowing blue caftan and pointed slippers. He towers a foot above Mike and me and the driver. He has a handsome, calm face with three deep cicatrices on each cheek. He puts one giant hand on my shoulder and one on Mike's.

"Gentlemen, you are wrong."

We protest but he shakes his head.

"This driver is not trying to cheat you." He speaks English with a French accent. "The driver must carry not only you, but your bags. Your bags are as heavy as you are."

He points to the wheels of the minivan. They are half flat and sunk up inside the wheel wells.

"Like all of us, you must buy tickets for yourselves *and* tickets for your bags."

The moment we comply, the driver pats our arms happily and jumps in and fires up the Toyota and begins rolling away honking.

The peacemaker has already compressed himself back inside.

Mike and I are trying to say good-bye to Rick and John, trying to say something right and meaningful because it is that moment when the river splits for good and forever, but it doesn't happen. All we can do is shake hands and wish them luck. They're waving and we're waving and the minivan is grinding off down the dirt road and we run and leap and a dozen hands pull us inside through the sliding door.

Our expedition is over.

It is a rough, fourteen-hour ride through the veld. Mike and I don't know it, but this will be our last bus ride in Africa together.

At first we both must stand. Bent over, hitting our heads on every bump, our faces four inches from other faces, our arms and legs laced between their arms and legs. Then, at a stop where there is nothing but desert, one man pries

172

himself out and Mike gets to sit down. The seat is so far in the back I can't see him.

No one else gets off until we reach the outskirts of Bamako. We pass through nine police checkpoints. At the Malian border all the passengers must pay the police but Mike and I have our paper from the Malian embassy. We show it to the commander. He doesn't understand why we are traveling like common Africans, but we pay nothing.

I must stand the whole way, curled over like a hunchback. After several hours I begin to get cramps. The passengers have been where I am and came prepared. They ply me with oranges, give me sips from their water bottles. A woman from the back hands up a small square of chocolate. When I fall into a painful sleep, the passengers around me hold me up.

We rock to a stop at one A.M. The door slides open. The minivan is so packed you would think we would all explode out like soda in a can that has been violently shaken, but we can't. We are dovetailed together. Only one person at a time can be detached. When it is my turn, the passengers behind me give me a push but my legs have been gone for hours and I fall out on my face in the dirt.

"It has been a long ride." I am being lifted up by the elbows by the giant peacemaker. He dusts me off and introduces himself.

"Kourou Nekoumba." He puts out a hand as large as a ham.

Mike and I give our names and shake his hand.

"And what are you two doing in Bamako?"

"I am going home," says Mike.

"I am going to Timbuktu."

I hadn't told Michael but he'd already figured it out. He slaps me on the back and grins.

"I see. And where are you two staying tonight?"

We don't know.

"Then you shall stay in my home." He turns and walks into the dark.

We aren't sure if we are supposed to follow him or not. We still have to get our bags down off the minivan.

He reappears pushing a taxi. The cabby is sitting inside. The car is so jury-rigged with mismatched parts it is impossible to determine its make or model. We load our gear on top and then push it down the road until the engine fires and we can hop in.

We limp through a maze of back roads. The taxi has only one headlight and it goes out when we hit bumps. There are no streetlamps. If you were to fly over Bamako at night, you would not know that there were a million souls below you. After an hour we stop outside a wall with a blue door.

Kourou pays the driver and bangs on the door. It creaks open and we follow him inside, dragging our gear. It is too dark and we are too tired to tell where we are. Kourou helps us put up our tent, wishes us a good night, and vanishes. We sleep and feel safe in our sleep and dream little.

The next day we will discover we are inside a small cement courtyard. There is a well in the middle and several orange trees. Surrounding the courtyard are attached cement apartments, each with a metal door and a window. Behind the door are two rooms; one with the window onto the courtyard and a windowless back bedroom whose rear wall forms the perimeter of the compound. Facilities are communal— along the entrance are two doors that open onto two roofless concrete closets. Both have holes in the floor. The one with the bucket is the shower; the one with the tin can, the toilet.

When we awake, it is already very warm and the compound is bustling all around us. We are embarrassed, as if we were tramps sleeping on someone's stoop. Women in swaths of bright cloth are squatting just outside their front doors cooking breakfast over charcoal fires, babies are crying, kids are playing chase, men have already left for work.

When Kourou sees us sit up, he rises from a broken wire chair in the corner and approaches our tent. In the light of day he looks just as big as he did at night, but much younger. By his manner we thought he was older than we are, but he is not.

"Breakfast is ready, gentlemen."

We slip on our clothes with all the kids staring and the women trying not to and walk across to Kourou's quarters.

"This is Fali, my wife."

A tall woman in a flowing purple caftan is bent over a butane burner on the ground. Her back is horizontal, one hand on her hip, legs spraddled like a giraffe. She is stirring something with one arm, the bracelets fallen over her hand. When she straightens up, we see why she was not squatting. It would be uncomfortable. She is pregnant.

Fali smiles shyly. She has a small head with cornrowed hair and a turned-up nose. She shakes our hands.

"*Bienvenus, voyageurs. Bienvenus dans notre maison.*"

The door to their apartment is half open and Kourou guides us inside and pushes us onto a low couch. There is a blanket over the window and the coolness of darkness settles over us. The room is tiny, no bigger than a cell, and smells of sweat. A tapestry of the holy city of Mecca hangs on the wall, nothing more. Set on a bench are three plates and two loaves of French bread. On the plates are omelettes with onions and cheese. Kourou sits down on a chair across from us, his knees up in his face.

"We eat together first, then talk."

During breakfast Mike and I can't help glancing out the doorway at Fali. We watch her pregnant body. She holds her shoulders back to counterbalance the weight, rubs the small of her back. She answers the calls and laughter of the other women in the compound. They are teasing her because she has toobob guests.

The moment we are finished, she steps inside with glasses of cold juice. I don't know how she has obtained it. There are no refrigerators in the compound. We tell her the food was wonderful and try to get her to sit down and drink the juice with us but she only smiles, turns her head away, and waves us off.

Kourou urges us to empty our glasses.

"Now we can talk."

Kourou wants to know everything. Where we come from and what we were doing in Siguiri and what we think of Africa and what we think of Africans. When we don't give complete enough or detailed enough answers, he probes us with more questions. After we have talked about Africa, we talk about America and after that about all places and all men. We talk with Kourou for hours before suddenly realizing we need to get into Bamako to buy Mike a plane ticket.

Kourou cannot go with us. He says he has business he must do. He gives us detailed directions on how to catch the right bus into Bamako and the right bus back out, how to exchange money on the black market and with whom, how to find our way to the airline ticket office, how to get past the security guards.

On a continent where nothing ever goes smoothly, it all goes smoothly. We return to the compound at dusk, ticket in hand. Tomorrow afternoon, Mike will fly home.

Dinner is waiting for us. Fali has created a feast. A mountain of couscous with meat and yams and carrots and peppers and apples and bananas. She tries to slip out but this time we won't let her. We tell her we will not eat unless she eats with us. Kourou smiles and the scars on his cheeks fold up. We all eat together with our hands.

Again Mike and I try not to watch Fali but we can't help ourselves. She is what we are missing. We told her our wives were pregnant. She knows we are staring at her but she graciously ignores us.

We eat as much as we can and are exhorted to eat more. We do our best but finally must stop. Fali pushes herself to her feet. She bends over to take the platter and we try to help her but she won't let us. We try anyway and she stops and her eyes fall on us and she speaks.

"*Je suis contente que vous soyez ici avec moi mais vous devriez être à la maison avec vos femmes.*"

We're not sure what she said. She repeats it, half in French, half in English: She is very glad we are here but we should be home with our wives not here with her.

I flash with guilt. Mike nods solemnly.

Mike is so homesick I have to steel myself not to let it infect me. I have to constantly remind myself that Mike and Diana have an understanding different from Sue's and mine. Diana expects Mike to be thinking about her and her struggles while he is away and to come home at the first opportunity. And he always does. Sue expects me to do whatever it is I think I must do.

Fali returns and passes out chocolate cookies, then eases herself back down into the chair beside Kourou and listens sleepily while Mike and Kourou converse.

Mike talks easily and happily the way you do when you know you don't have to live up to anything anymore. What you wanted to do you have done and everything from here on out is downhill.

Then the teapot begins to sing. Fali rises to her feet and steps outside into the moonlight. She looks up at the stars.

When she comes back, she is carrying a tray with a teapot and four glasses. Kourou lifts the swanlike vessel and pours and the fluid drops cleanly into the glasses.

Then, once again, the supplication.

"*À la vie. À la mort. À l'amour.*" To life. To death. To love.

The hot sweet liquid burning our throats.

We stepped off the ship in Sicily and rejoiced. As we knew it would, our journey in Africa immediately began to take on mythical proportions. While we were there, it hadn't always seemed so grand, but we knew better. When you're right in the thick of it, sometimes the best way to get through with a grin is just to imagine what a great story it will make. Mike and I had perfected this stratagem to an art.

We were still without possessions. We had decided being robbed was the best thing that could have happened. It was

177

as if some cowboy had popped the slipknot and the saddle and saddlebags and blankets had dropped to the ground. We bolted into Europe bucking and kicking.

Florence to see the statue of David. Dachau to experience guilt, briefly. Paris because it was warm now. Amsterdam for the blondes. Up to the Arctic Circle. Over to Russia where we sold our jeans on the black market and were once again arrested.

We bivouacked every night on church stoops and under park benches and spent the days roaming through different countries living cheek by jowl with misfits, runaways, orphans, and crazies. Europe turned out not to be so tame after all.

One day our money ran out. Every cent. But by now we were pros. We knew all the tricks.

A month later we were hopping trains and found a wallet on a bench in a German train station. The wallet was fat with bills. Enough money to keep us going for years. We debated, the way you do when you're tempted:

Guy didn't need it as bad as we did because if he did he wouldn't have had so much. Finders keepers, losers weepers. Guy's probably so filthy rich he wouldn't even miss it.

Eventually our pride kicked in and when a conductor walked by, we handed him the billfold.

"That was good of you."

We spun around. There was a woman seated beside a bearded man on the bench back-to-back with ours. They had overheard our whole conversation.

"It was the right thing to do," said the man.

We didn't know what to say. No one respectable ever spoke to us.

"Where are you going?" asked the woman.

We answered at the same time. Mike said everywhere and I said nowhere.

"I see." She smiled. "And have you been to Kronenberg?"

They took us there, to their home. A tiny immaculate

apartment overlooking a flowered courtyard. We slept in clean sheets. We took showers twice a day using up all the hot water. We sat in chairs and ate toast from clean plates. We walked barefoot on warm wooden floors. We listened to music from a stereo. We looked at books on oak bookshelves.

It had been so long, we'd forgotten this life. We had been living outdoors for months. We had become annealed. We had become nomads.

One evening she said, "Don't you miss your home?"

We were cleanscrubbed and cleanshaven sitting on their black couch in clean clothes drinking a glass of French wine listening to Bach. I remember I was staring at an Escher print on the wall. There was a stream zigzagging up a channel, spilling over a waterfall, then going back up again.

We both said no.

"No?"

We did. We did so much we couldn't even talk about it. Our homesickness was hidden inside us like a key we had swallowed. We never talked about it because we were still young and embarrassed and believed homesickness was a sign of weakness rather than love.

We touched down at JFK less than a week later. Mike and I split up there. We already had our next trip planned. Enough of people and cities and pollution and culture. We were going back to the mountains where we belonged. We were going back to Alaska to climb Mount McKinley.

We shook hands. Mike was taking a bus north to Cape Cod to see a girlfriend. I was hitchhiking out across the wilderness of America. We'd hook back up in Wyoming.

We shook hands again, then suddenly hugged each other, sad and uncomfortable, ending softly what had started out so big so long before, not yet knowing that this is the way all journeys end. You can never go home again, and you always do.

The following afternoon, 9 November 1991, a taxi tilts in through the hollows of dirt outside the compound.

Kourou and Fali are dressed up for the occasion. Kourou is wearing a knee-length embroidered tunic and billowing pants, both satin white. He looks like a giant prince in pajamas. Fali is wreathed in an elegant purple and black caftan with a matching turban.

The four of us ride out to the airport together.

Mike checks in the bags. He is taking my boat home with him. He is wearing a new shirt he bought in Bamako and clean trousers that Fali washed by hand. He looks the way he has not looked during our entire expedition in Africa, respectable. Because of this our bags are not searched. They roll innocently up the conveyor belt, the Ruger never fired for any reason other than boredom.

Kourou and Fali say good-bye. Kourou shakes Mike's hand and looks gravely down on him and Fali hugs him over her stomach.

"*Bon voyage. Ta femme sera heureuse de te voir.*"

They go outside and leave the two of us alone.

We jump up onto a deserted counter and resume palavering. We have been talking all day. We are planning our next adventure.

Enough of water. Next year it's back to the mountains. The Himalayas. Not the front country. Not Nepal or Kathmandu or Lhasa. The back side of Tibet. Someplace farther away and more unknown.

We are mapping it out, brainstorming, strategizing, plotting, firing possibilities back and forth, pros and cons, all the stuff we love—when Mike stops short.

"What?"

He's grinning at the floor.

"What?"

"We haven't changed, have we?"

"Yes, we have. You're going home, aren't you?"

"You know what I mean."

"We can't."

"We could."

"I don't think so. We don't want to."

"We should."

"Yes, I know."

"Maybe we'll want to."

"Maybe we'll want to, but we won't be able to."

The loudspeaker announces Mike's flight in French. I cannot pass through security. I give him an envelope. It is a long letter to Sue needlessly explaining why I am staying when Mike is coming home.

We hug each other and say good-bye. It is not a difficult good-bye because we know we will see each other back home in Wyoming. We have a lifetime of journeys left to do together. We plan to raise our kids together. Teach them how to ride bikes. Take them camping. Teach them how to misadventure properly.

This is the faith of living. To move through life as though it will always be there. To see the future as something as solid and wonderful as the present.

Mike passes through the gates, turns, throws his arms in the air, and tosses me his outrageous grin.

It is evening when Fali and Kourou and I return to the compound. Inside the walls the courtyard is alive. The women are cooking upon their small fires and gabbing and the men have set a cracked TV on a chair and are watching a soccer match and the children have a puppy whose growling is making them giggle. Fali joins the women. Kourou greets the guys but walks past them to a moped slumped against the wall. I follow him as he wheels it out of the compound.

Kourou cranes over the little vehicle and adjusts some things and then squats onto the seat and starts pedaling. He is so big and the moped so small he looks like a circus bear on a bicycle. The toy engine coughs and sputters and finally stays alive and he makes several circles before pulling up beside me.

"Mark, I have business I must do now."

I still don't know what Kourou does for a living. Whenever I have inquired, he has been cryptic.

"Every man must have his business. Without his business he cannot live. Without his business he cannot be a man."

When I asked why he was on the bus in Siguiri, he said he had gone to Guinea to search for gold. Last night he said he had lived in Saudi Arabia and worked on oil derricks. All I have gathered is he is an entrepreneur. Like Sori Keita, like all Africans.

He is holding the throttle and the engine is bawling.

"What is your business, Kourou?"

He grins and nods over his shoulder. I swing on and sit down.

The moped is like a burro. I'm surprised we don't break its back. Kourou's knees almost touch the handlebars. His giant slippers droop off the pegs. He guns the motor and we begin to move.

We do not take the paved road into Bamako. We ride through the waves of dirt that surround the city, passing one concrete compound after another. In the streets there are children shining with dust and boys playing soccer with a flat ball and piles of garbage with rats sitting on top like gophers. Kourou's clothes waft back around me like a sail.

As we leave the compounds, he begins to speak. He doesn't look back over his shoulder.

"In Africa a man cannot do his business on a bus. The buses are too slow. The buses do not go where his business wants to go."

We are entering the bush. The sky and the dirt and the air are all the color of an apricot. I hold myself up when we strike bumps.

"But a car is too expensive. The African man cannot have a car."

When we first talked about America, Kourou asked if it was true what he saw in videos, that everyone, even young boys and girls, owned a car. We were sitting in his concrete cell and I felt the profligacy of my nation and told him not everybody had a car, but he knew better. He said he didn't need a car. He said he wanted a motorcycle. That was his dream.

We come upon a herd of sheep grazing on bedrock. Two small girls are among them. Their eyes follow us as we cleave their flock.

Past the sheep the wheels of the moped crack against a stone step and the frame shudders.

"It wouldn't matter anyway," cries Kourou. "Our roads are no good for a car. In Africa we have moto. The moto is the new feet of the African man."

Mike and I had seen this for ourselves in downtown Bamako. The entire city was whizzing with mopeds. Bakery delivery boys with baskets big as barrels, schoolgirls, men in suits with briefcases, whole families balanced like acrobats on one tiny machine.

"But there is a problem. A moto needs petrol. The petrol is controlled by the government. The government is rich people, so, of course, sometimes there is no petrol for the poor people. But when they have no petrol they cannot do their business and when they cannot do their business their families do not eat."

The trail we are following intersects a highway. We ride up onto the asphalt and turn south. In the dirt we were going slow enough that I could hear him but now the engine is screaming and he doesn't talk.

A few miles into the desert we come upon a dozen tractor trailers grouped on a knoll just off the highway. Against the skyline they look like prehistoric animals. There is nothing here. No gas station, no café, no building of any kind.

I tell Kourou I can walk but he forces the moped up the hill. We ride slowly through the sleeping hulks. The drivers are lying in the dark under the bellies of their beasts, greasy and puffeyed, drinking beer and eating. We stop beside a petrol truck.

"Please wait here."

Kourou steps off and walks over to a man sleeping near the rear axles. He throws a stone at the man and the man wakes up cursing and Kourou laughs and the man laughs when he sees who it is. Kourou sits down beside him beneath the tank of the truck and they talk. I see Kourou take something from his pocket and give it to the man. Then he comes back and gets on and starts the moped by pedaling us down off the hill. We zoom onto the highway.

"Did it go well?" I am shouting in the dark.

"Yes."

When we get back to the village, we do not stop at the compound but slope on by in the moonlight. A mile away we pull up to a mud hut sitting back from the street. Kourou produces a key and unlocks the padlock on the door. Inside it is pitch dark. I don't know why he doesn't light a candle. After my eyes adjust, I see there is nothing in the hut but fifty-five-gallon drums and a stack of two-stroke oil jugs. The fifty-five-gallon drums are dented and patched with crude welds.

Kourou takes a cudgel from the wall and begins hitting the barrels. There are nine of them. Seven of them boom hollowly; two make dull flat sounds. Kourou picks up two stones from the ground near the door and places them on the full barrels. Stepping back outside, he closes the door and slips the padlock through the metal ring but doesn't relock it.

On the ride home we stop at a *boulangerie*. The window is lit up by blue and red lights. Kourou is in high spirits. He selects two of the most expensive pastries.

"One for Fali, one for the baby."

The compound is asleep by the time we get back. I hold the door and Kourou wheels his moped inside. I am hoping we will pull the chairs out into the courtyard and Kourou will explain to me what I have seen today but he simply wishes me good-night.

When I try to ask a question, he says, "In the morning."

He wakes me in my tent at dawn. We quietly roll the moped outside and get it started and ride to the mud hut. The padlock is locked. He unlocks it and we step inside. Panels of dusty pink light fall through the mud roof. Kourou hits each barrel and they all thud. As we step out, a boy of perhaps fifteen is approaching. Kourou hands him the key and padlock and they talk for a few minutes before we leave.

Kourou takes us back to the *boulangerie*. It has already reopened. He shuts his moped off and orders four pastries.

He hands me the first two, putting one in each hand, and takes the second two for himself. We set out on a walk through the rolling dirt streets of the compound. It is still early but people are already up. Mopeds are scooting about. Their riders wave at Kourou and shout, "*Bonjour. Bonjour.*"

"You have figured it out, Mark?"

"Almost."

Kourou didn't use to have a moped. He used to walk, like all Africans. One day he was fishing in the river and the fishing was not good so he went farther down the bank. He discovered the barrels abandoned in the mud along the water. One by one, each barrel taking one day, he rolled them back to his village. He rolled them directly to a welder who made them sound again. He got the money to rent the hut from his uncle.

The petrol comes from Nigeria. The tanks on the tractor trailers can hold several more barrels than their registered capacity. The truck drivers pay off the men who fill the tanks. Kourou buys the excess from the truckers. They fill up his barrels in the middle of the night before lumbering into Bamako, where the police inspect them to ensure that they are still carrying their stated capacity. Kourou sells the petrol at a cut rate to the people in his village. The boy works for Kourou. He is the serviceman. He screws off the cap, pours in a gulp of two-stroke oil, then sucks on the tube until the petrol splashes into the hungry stomach of the moped.

A couple of days later Kourou and I take the bus into Bamako. We sit together on a narrow bench, Kourou's knees smashed into the seat in front of us. The bus stops for everyone and becomes packed with humans but the driver continues to stop for everyone and they all get on.

The city thickens around us. By the time we cross the bridge over the Niger and enter Bamako proper, the air is viscous with blue fumes and traffic has stalled. Only two-wheeled vehicles are moving. The nimble and the quick.

Mopeds, bicycles, motorcycles, people on foot—all streaming around us as if we were on a boulder in a river.

We get off the bus and are swept away by humanity.
Kourou knows where we're going. He is a head taller than
everyone. He takes me by the hand and we begin threading
through the anarchy of free enterprise—shops and shacks
and street vendors all crushed together selling everything
there is on earth. Used car parts, used bike parts, used
plumbing supplies, pyramids of oranges, purses, black
market Levi's, doughnuts, magazines, canned goods, ice
cream, refrigerators, books, washing machines, tattoos.

After half an hour we pass out of the commercial district
into the industrial zone. Ten minutes later we turn a corner
and step into an inferno of labor and combustion. Hundreds
of grease-smeared boys all bent over motorcycles welding
or pounding or tightening, patching tires, blowing through
carburetors or greasing bearings or tying electrical wires
with permanently stained hands. The noise is terrific. The
boys are so enraptured they do not notice us.

At the end of the alley on the corner is a store with a big
glass window. There is a motorcycle in the window. It is red
and shines as bright as a Christmas ornament.

Kourou opens the door and closes it behind us. At the
counter is a fat little man. He is from India but speaks to us
in Bambara. I know he knows English but he ignores me and
talks with Kourou. Kourou does the bargaining. In a matter
of minutes, I am the owner of the motorcycle in the window.

Kourou swings the door wide open and I push the gleam-
ing machine out onto the crowded sidewalk. I am surprised
by its weight. All the muscle of steel. Kourou is watching
me. He is as jubilant as I am.

He tries to refuse but I insist. He grips the handlebars
and swings on and kicks the starter all in one fluid motion,
as if he has been practicing it in his dreams. On the second
try the motorcycle comes alive and he throttles it carefully.
I climb on behind him, put my arms around his waist, and
we roll away.

We ride back down motorcycle alley through the crowd

of boys. This time they stop what they are doing, look up, and admire the gorgeous new machine in their midst.

When we get to the main thoroughfare, traffic is still hopelessly clogged. We lift our legs, slide the motorbike between two bumpers, turn into the aisle between two lanes of stalled vehicles, and Kourou guns it.

We are flying down the corridor between the lines of buses and trucks and taxis. I catch the faces of the people trapped behind smudgy windshields. If anyone were to open his door, we would be catapulted into space and killed. But we are not thinking about this. We are not thinking at all. We are riding. The trip into town took us two hours; we make it back out in twenty minutes.

Kourou brings Fali into the street with her hands over her eyes. When she lifts them, she gasps. She cannot believe what we have done. She awkwardly leans forward and reads.

"*Ya-ma-ha cent-vingt-cinq.*"

She says she doesn't want a ride and touches her stomach. But I must give her a ride. Sue would go for a ride. She would get on behind me and put her arms around my waist and pull herself close and I would feel the firm roundness against the small of my back.

Fali straddles the bike and fastens her arms around me. We ride the swells of the dirt outside the compound. We circle the block and the children wave and run after us. I give it gas just for her to see what it can do and she hugs me tighter and shrieks, "*Merde!*"

When I drop Fali off, there is already a crowd of kids waiting. I give rides until I'm out of gas. Each child clings to me like a frightened monkey but wants another ride the moment I stop.

The next day Kourou and I return to Bamako. We ride together on my bike back to the alley of hope and creation and find a boy with a welding machine. His gloves are so big for him I can't believe he can do the job.

Kourou explains what we want and the boy listens intently. He shows us to a tangled pile of used motorcycle racks. I choose one that is small and heavy. The boy takes it and holds it extended behind the saddle and looks at me to see if that is what I want. I nod. We leave my motorcycle with him. When I look over my shoulder, he already has the seat off.

I will be in the desert so I will have to be self-sufficient. I need some tools but I'm not exactly sure which ones. I know a lot about bicycles, but I was twelve the last time I rode a motorcycle.

Kourou helps me. We buy wrenches and pliers and screwdrivers of various sizes and types for the various bolts and screws on the bike. A twenty-liter plastic container for extra petrol. A five-liter jug of two-stroke oil. A tire patch kit. Spare tubes of grease. Spare spark plug. Rubber straps to tie my backpack onto the rack.

After two hours we return to the boy mechanic. He is working on another motorcycle. My bike is off to the side. The rack has been welded on so square and solid it looks as if it had always been there.

We ride together out of the city. This time I am steering and Kourou is on the back holding on to me. We know it is our last ride together. We don't talk. We don't go fast. We let the motorcycle carry us.

Kourou insists that we stop at his hut. He fills my tank and then the twenty-liter fuel container until the gas is running down the sides. I try to pay him but he won't take my money. He knows I so much want to do something for him. I have tried to talk to him about it several times. After he has locked up the hut, he turns to me.

"Mark, someday you will not be traveling. Someday you will be in your home and someone else will be traveling. They will need you and you will help them."

Riding back to the compound I stop at a grocery store and buy two large canisters of whole milk. It is all that I can think of to give Fali. She will not accept anything from me that is for her. I have already tried. But milk. She will know that it is not for her, but for her child. All she must do is drink it.

When we arrive at the compound, I place the canisters of milk in her arms. She knows now that I am leaving.

"*Pourquoi dois-tu partir?*" She doesn't understand. Why must I go? Why? Do I want to leave?

I tell her I don't want to leave but I want to go.

She shakes her head. It makes no sense to her.

I say I must go.

She peers into me as if searching for something at the bottom of a pool. I look away. It is not her eyes. It is her body. Her body shames me. The round warm weight of the life within her presses the will out of me. Makes me question every minute I have been away.

"*Non.*" She clicks her tongue. "*Non.*"

She says I was right the first time. I *want* to go. I do not *have* to go.

"*Ton envie de partir est plus fort que ton envie de rester.*"

Your desire to leave is greater than your desire to stay.

I hesitate, then say simply, "*Oui.*"

I have been forced to admit this before. Sue has forced me. Each time before I leave she makes me admit that expeditions are selfish. She wants it made clear. I used to argue. Contrive defenses trying to prove that my leaving for months was good for both of us. Then I would feel guilty and declare that this was the last time and after this one it was over and I wouldn't go again and she would say, "Mark, be honest with yourself, would you? I am."

Sue and I don't go through this anymore. When people say it is easier to be honest, they don't mean with other people. They mean with yourself.

Fali says she has found out about this place called Timbuktu. She has ears. She can read. *C'est dangereux. Il y a la guerre.* The Tuaregs are attacking the Bambara. They come out of the desert on camels and steal trucks and then the Bambara send black helicopters into the sands to kill the Tuaregs.

I don't argue with her because what she has learned is true. Instead I tell her I will be careful.

She laughs. "*Même si tu fais attention, cela ne dépend pas de toi.*" You cannot be careful. It is not up to you.

It is another argument I lost long ago.

Kourou speaks to her. He tells her it is my business that is taking me away. He says I am a man. I have my own business like all men.

Fali looks hard at me. It is not a cruel look. It is sorrow. She passes through the doorway cradling the two canisters of milk in her arms like twins.

René Caillie lit out for Africa when he was sixteen. An orphan boy apprenticed to the cobbler in the village of Mauze, France, he had become impassioned by reading books. *Robinson Crusoe* was the last straw. He stepped into a new pair of shoes, hid the sixty francs he had saved in his belt, kissed his crippled sister good-bye, and walked out of town.

The year was 1816. He sailed from France to the west coast of Africa. No place on earth was more pestilent. In Freetown, a city where he would later spend over a year, 1,421 of its 1,658 white residents perished from disease. Caillie, a slip of a boy, thrived. The French and the English were fighting a war over West Africa. Gold, ostrich feathers, ivory, indigo, amber, black market slaves. Caillie could not care less. He set out on foot, exploring up and down the coast.

He heard about the deaths of Major Peddie and Captain Campbell and their disastrous Timbuktu expedition. When their replacements, William Gray and military surgeon John Dochard, put out word for fresh recruits, Caillie hiked 150 miles to join up. He arrived upon bloody feet, ragged and starved, and was told he was unacceptable.

Dejected, he sailed to the West Indies where he read Mungo Park's *Travels in the Interior of Africa*. The West Indies were too civilized anyway. Back to Africa.

By this time, 1819, the Gray/Dochard expedition had splintered. Gray was held captive by a chief and the whereabouts of the Dochard contingent was unknown. A man named Partarrieu was chosen to lead a relief expedition. Caillie pestered the man until he acquiesced. It was a messy, eighteen-month journey into the interior. Many close calls, many deaths. Gray and Dochard made it back alive, albeit with severe dysentery. Partarrieu too, although with hookworm. Caillie stumped out of the jungle with malaria.

Destitute and diseased, he found work as a cook in a coastal factory, staying just long enough to earn passage home. Back in France he spent the next four years quietly working for a wine merchant, saving his money, honing his plan.

Caillie was perceptive. He recognized big expeditions for what they were: inefficient, ineffective, and deadly. Contrary to common consensus, there was no safety in numbers. More men, more beasts, and more gear would not increase security or one's chances for success. Just the opposite. The more one had, the more one was worth attacking. To Caillie, there was only one way to safely penetrate Africa: alone, traveling light. Instead of more accouterments, what was needed was more knowledge. The English marched into Africa in velvet waistcoats and linen britches quoting the Bible and firing bullets. No wonder they died. They knew nothing of Muslim mores, language, culture, or religion.

In 1824, Caillie returned to Africa and walked straight into the flaming Sahara. He presented himself before the Braknas nomads, a fanatical Muslim tribe of almost pure Moor blood. The Braknas were renowned for their cruelty, their filthiness, and their intense hatred of Christians. Caillie claimed to be an apostate and wished to be rigorously tutored in Islam. He was put under the supervision of a merciless marabout.

For a year Caillie lived the life of a Muslim ascetic. He tramped in thin leather sandals through thorns and scorching wastelands, slept in his djellaba, curled up like an animal during sandstorms. His only food was porridge and sour milk. He learned to read and write Arabic. He trained himself to chant lengthy passages from the Koran by heart.

He disciplined himself to endure privation. Hunger, thirst, exhaustion, pain. When he reappeared out of the desert, burned black by the sun, he was ready.

He petitioned first the French and then the English to support his journey to Timbuktu. He was refused by both. The French had already sent out Beaufort. The English had Laing trekking south from Tripoli and Clapperton pushing north from Nigeria.

Once again Caillie was broke. This time he refused to return to France. He was offered a job in a Freetown indigo factory and began again to save his pennies and prepare for his journey.

Caillie was fastidious. He knew he would need to understand distance. To this end, after work he began walking briskly for several hours along a road with mile markers, teaching himself to gauge speed, to feel in his legs how far he had gone. He would also need to navigate without map or compass; he practiced taking bearings from the sun during the day and the stars at night. He would have to speak the language of the non-Arabic traders—he took to spending every evening with the local Malinke merchants, learning not only their tongue, but their duplicity in barter.

After a year Caillie quit his job. He had saved 2,000 francs. He figured it was more than enough. He was pleased he had not received sponsorship. He would be free, beholden to no one. Besides, he had recently learned of the 10,000-franc prize offered by the French Geographical Society to the first man to reach Timbuktu and return alive. He planned to be that man. He would give the money to his crippled sister.

For his journey he bought silver and gold, gunpowder, amber, coral, tobacco, knives, scissors, and beads—all of which fit into a leather rucksack along with the Koran and his compass. The day of his departure he slipped from his European dress and donned the rough, soiled djellaba of the nomadic Moor. He buried his native religion and professed only one God, Allah. He hid away his native tongue and from that moment on spoke only Arabic or Malinke.

René Caillie vanished. In his place was Abd Allahi.

Abd Allahi had been born of Arabian parents in Egypt. When he was a child, his parents had been killed by Napoleon's soldiers. He was taken to France and later sold as a slave to a merchant from Senegal. Back in Africa he had so pleased his master that after some years he had been given his freedom. Now his only desire was to cross Africa and return to his homeland of Egypt.

It was March 1827. Beaufort was dead. Laing was dead. Clapperton would die in a month. René Caillie, twenty-six, was setting out for Timbuktu alone.

Before dawn, when the sky is only beginning to promise itself, we roll the motorcycle out of the compound. The street is deserted. Kourou helps me load up. I hold the bike while he doubles the rubber straps, using all his weight to bind my backpack and the fuel containers onto the rack.

I tromp the kick starter and the motorcycle wakes like a deer sprung to its feet.

Kourou has already hugged me and shaken my hand and squeezed my shoulder. Fali puts both arms around my neck, squeezes hard, and lets go.

I think I should not look back but I do. Kourou has his head tilted upward and his arms folded on his chest. He is breathing in the twilight. Fali is standing beside him, one arm resting on the shelf of her stomach, the other stretched up in the air waving.

I lean the bike, turn the corner.

The motorcycle bears me away. Over the bridge, through Bamako before it is even awake, off the end of the pavement into the desert.

For the next ten days I follow a thread of cart tracks and footpaths on the north side of the Niger. Sometimes the route is confusing, like the paw prints of a fox, but I find my way. This is what a motorcycle can do. In this sense a motor-cycle is like a kayak. A sleek, independent vehicle. A craft capable of perceiving and then following the most evanes-cent path.

I ride through Koulikoro and Doumba and Sirakola. Through Banamba and Nyamima and Farako. Sansanding to Kolongotomo, Massina to Monimpebougou. I do not go in a straight line. I go anywhere I want—over, across, zigzag, circle back.

Each village rises up out of the white-brown plain improbable as an island in the ocean. But then there are islands in the ocean, and people find them, and build them-selves homes and stay.

I motor in between the mud walls. Past the whitewashed mosque with crescent and star and an ostrich egg glinting in the furnace of the sky. Past the cracking mud well with a bucket sewn from a truck inner tube. Through the scattering bleating sheep and goats and kids.

I stop in the shade of an acacia to let the engine cool. Dismount, lift my sunglasses. I am coated with the desert. My eyes are a raccoon's.

In the middle of every village is a square. In the square there is sometimes a market. Stands with plastic sheeting held up as shields against the spears of sun. Fruit canoed down the Niger. Cones of dried peppers. Piles of sheep parts heavy with flies. A table with scissors and scythes. In between the stands, out in the burning dirt, are the living things. Camels and ducks and donkeys, girls balancing water, hard-knuckled boys, hooded men, turbaned women with faces black as oil.

I am thirsty, sometimes hungry, saddle-sore. I take walks through these tiny communities and eat while I'm walking. Dates, oranges, dried fish.

Somewhere in the village I find a barrel in the shade beside a mud hut, oil stains in the dirt. I push my motorcycle to the hut and pay the boy. He sucks on the tube and fills my tanks and I put on my sunglasses and ride away.

At night I ride under the silver moonlight through great empty spaces. I glide through dishes of green sand fine as flour. Over bedrock solid right through to the other side of the earth. Around solitary baobab trees, the immense lumpy hearts of the desert, their polyped, tuberous arms plugged so deep into the night sky I imagine a well within every one.

When I get tired, I stop and get off, swig water, and stretch. Take a walk and breathe in the silent coolness of the desert at dark. Then I lay out my sleeping bag beside my motorcycle and lie down and watch the stars and let my eyes close.

I rise long before dawn to escape the heat of the day and plunge into the lavender place between sky and earth.

I ride upright in the saddle, my arms before me, my hands grasping the handlebars. The motorcycle is warm between my legs and the engine purrs. My feet rest on the metal pegs just above the moving ground and my thighs absorb the dips. I move as one with my machine through the gloaming. It is natural. As if I have been riding a motorcycle since I was a boy.

I can feel the slipstream behind me, the cleaved open space that my movement is slicing through the air. But I also feel the slipstream around me, as if I am inside my own slipstream. I understand this means I must simultaneously be before myself, forcibly splitting the air, and behind myself gliding in my own velvet wake, and I am. Such is a pilgrimage.

Then a crack appears at the end of the desert. The sun is to rise. When it does, I will no longer be a phantom moving swift and shadowless over the flesh of the desert. Lavender will become light and duality will begin.

The sun pulls itself up onto the horizon and soaks me in red and creates for me my shadow. At first it is behind me, trying to catch up. But it gains quickly, moving out to my side and becoming my companion.

I am small and compact but my shadow is amazing. There is so much space my shadow does not look like me. Only when I drop into a gully and the land is suddenly close does it spring forward and become my size, but then I ride out again and it expands at once, bursting confinement, stretching the length of the desert.

For a moment—for that is all we are ever given—I leave myself and become my shadow. My head ten feet tall, my knees huge angles, my arms great arcs. I become a flickering cave painting, the myth of myself.

Then the sun lifts far above me and I squeeze down to a tiny dot moving across the desert.

The engine is acting up again. Yesterday it coughed off and on but I thought it was just bad gasoline. I considered stopping and having a look but didn't because I was in the middle of nowhere and it might not start once I shut it off.

Now it's again catching and jerking. According to the map I should have reached the village an hour ago.

I am in a wadi with shelf rock above me to either side. I thought this was where the track went but now I am not sure. I steer off the gravel into the sand and up a slit in the rock. My bike begins to lurch and I try to keep it going but it dies just at the crest.

I hop off and rock the bike up onto the kickstand and gaze out into the desert. I see what I think might be something, three, maybe four miles away. Could be the village. Could be a band of rocks. Could be a mirage.

My bike refuses to come back to life even after I kick the starter repeatedly. Eventually I flood it and have to start pushing. The sand makes it much harder than I expected. I have to strain to move the bike at all. After a hundred yards I lean the machine against a boulder.

I have just gotten everything off my bike and dug out the tools when I hear a *clop clop clop* and spin around. There is a mule cart behind me. I have no idea where it came from. It draws up and stops.

The mule smells. A man and a boy are sitting on a wooden bench supported above the bed of the cart by car springs. The man peers down at me and the boy cocks his head up at the man. The man nods at the boy and the boy jumps down.

I am looking at the engine and the boy squats beside me and looks at the engine. I look at him. He looks at me. I smile. He smiles.

"*Salaam alaikum,*" I say. Welcome.

"*Allah akbar,*" says the boy. God is great.

The boy plunks the gas tank with his finger. We shake our heads together. I open the plastic compartment to check the oil tank but it too is full. The boy taps me on the shoulder. He is gliding his palm smoothly over the ground then suddenly makes a fist, stops his hand, and grunts.

"*NN.*"

I shake my head.

He raises his hand and glides his palm slowly downward. "*NNNNNNnnnnnnnn . . .*"

I shake my head.

He holds his hand horizontally above the ground, this time moving it in small lunges. "*NNNNNN . . . NNNNNN . . . NNNNNN . . .*"

I nod.

He grins and picks out a tool from my kit. He touches the engine to make sure it is not hot, then goes to work. In several seconds he has the spark plug out and is holding it in his hand pointing at something with his finger. In the gap between the tip of the spark plug and the coil wire is a black crystal. He scrapes it out, replaces the spark plug and rolls up my tools.

The boy climbs back up onto the cart and sits down beside his father. I stomp the kick starter and my motorcycle comes instantly to life. The boy waves and the man slaps the hindquarters of the mule.

The days are so hot that one morning I get up at four. I think it is an early start but when I get to a well, the women are already there. They are in a circle clapping in harmony, taking turns bouncing their whole body weight on the big handle and shoving large plastic buckets beneath the invisible gushing.

They are surprised to see me, a man, awake. They are mothers. Mothers and their daughters who are mothers and their child daughters who will be mothers. They are standing with bare feet in shallow black pools of water. They stop clapping and pumping and laugh at the sight of a man awake at such an hour, their faces turning up to the starlight and their breasts shaking.

I shut off my motorcycle and get out my canteen. A small girl takes it from me. Someone pumps and she holds it under the phosphorescent splashing until it is overflowing. She brings it back to me. I thank her and put the bottle back into my pack and get back on my bike and the women resume clapping and pumping.

I have been alone and do not want to leave this sound, the coitaling of hands in the darkness. I sit on my motorcycle and listen.

It is not random clapping or even just hands smacking in unison, it is a song. There is melody and rhythm and syncopation. Solos leap from different women. It is complicated and beautiful.

But once the women have filled their buckets, they are done. The pump stops spilling out water and the clapping stops and the women turn to their buckets. Every woman and child must carry one bucket on her head and one in each hand, so they cannot clap.

They are moving off in single file into the desert and I am just about to start my bike when one of them begins singing. When the chorus comes around, they all join in.

A small dark object alone out in the immensity. I noticed it ten minutes ago. It was trembling in the golden heat and I couldn't tell what it was. Could have been a post or a stump. Now I am closer and I can see that it is a human.

We are on the same track on a plate of desert, puny as ants below the mouth of the sky. The figure is moving but I am too far away to know whether it is walking toward me or away from me.

It is a man, not a woman. I can see that now. He is walking toward me. We are eating the distance between us, I much faster than he.

The man has something on his head. At first I thought it was a hat but no, it is a small bundle.

I am coming up on him. I downshift and then stop. I shut off the engine and welcome the silence. Rock the motorcycle up onto the kickstand, flex my knees, spit through cracked lips, adjust the back of my turban to cover my neck.

He is moving swiftly so he also downshifts to slow himself. Pulls back the thrust of his body, stops his swinging arms, halts the snap of his legs.

"*Bonne journée, monsieur.*"

"Good day to you."

He is wearing Western clothes. A blue long-sleeve shirt, dusty trousers, what once were sneakers. Snakes of sweat slide out from under the small bundle on his head. His armpits are wet down to his waist.

"I spake Englis. Ahmoud Al-Kan Koumbi is my father. I am Ahmoud Afma Al-Kan Koumbi. I am fourteen years. I go to Mopti for to work rice. My uncle work rice. I want work rice. Where are you go, sir?"

"Timbuktu."

"Ah. You have hunger, sir?"

"No thank you."

He raises his arms and lifts the bundle off his head and sets it on the ground. He unties the knot in the leather and pulls the corners back. In the middle of the chamois is a spare cotton shirt. It too is blue, neatly folded. On top of the shirt is a calabash the size of a large grapefruit. It is half full. He raises it by the handle and holds it out to me.

This is all he has and he will need it but that means nothing in the desert. He has offered. I must not refuse.

I hold the bowl with both hands and lift it to my lips. I am not going to fake it. He is watching my throat. I take a big drink. It is millet porridge. Warm, acrid, foul, the camel milk long soured.

"Thank you."

"Sir."

I turn around and open the top of my pack. I have ten oranges. It is too many. I must not give too much. In the desert the obligation to return in kind is immutable, sometimes fatal. I lift out four and close the pack and squat beside him. I split each orange in two with my pocketknife, setting four halves before him, leaving four halves in front of myself. It is my offering and he cannot refuse.

We have a picnic, resting on our haunches, staring out into the shimmering distance. We eat slowly. You only eat fast when you have too much to eat. We eat with our right hands, lapping up the drips between our fingers before they perish in the sand. He wastes nothing. He gnaws at the pulp on the inside of the scraps until they are transparent.

It has not been perfectly equal. He is only fourteen but he is acutely aware of this. He pushes his calabash toward me but now I am not obligated to consume more of his food.

I unfold my map.

"Where are you from?"

He speaks the name of his village. I scan the map but have no idea how it is spelled. He swivels his head. The sweat has evaporated leaving tracks of salt down his cheeks and neck. I don't think he can read a map. I slide it over and point to approximately where we are. He nods. He moves his finger north to a small word in the blankness.

"Zemraguie?"

He nods and repeats the word but it sounds nothing like what I have said.

"It not my village. My village small walking to this place."

I ask him when he left his village. He says yesterday morning. I look on the map.

"You walked the whole way?"

"Sir. My uncle write letter. He tell Afma work rice good work. He tell Afma Mopti three days walking."

My eyes leave his and return to the map. I hold my thumb and forefinger in a pincer position on the scale, then measure the distance.

"Did you stop to sleep?"

"No. My uncle say three days walking."

"Did you stop at all?"

He smiles.

I have not been attentive. His calabash is half empty. He must have stopped to eat at least once. Probably several times, rationing himself.

He is reknotting his bundle. He stands up and places it back on top of his head.

"*Bon voyage, monsieur*." He shakes my hand softly. I can feel the rough calluses.

"Good-bye."

He strides away, quickly getting up to speed.

It is ten in the morning. He has been walking for twenty-eight hours and covered one hundred miles. Mopti is a hundred more.

One day my motorcycle journey ends.

On a desolate track winding through hills of sand a vehicle appears ahead of me. As we approach each other, it grinds off the trail. A hand comes out and flags me down. I pull alongside and stop.

It is a tan Land Cruiser with blue stripes and tinted windows, spare fuel tanks welded to the sides. The windows open. There are half a dozen soldiers inside holding rifles between their knees. They are wearing sunglasses. They speak to me in French. I don't understand much but they are clearly telling me I can go no farther.

I nod.

They keep talking to me and I catch only words. Something about shooting, killing. I am waiting for them to drive on. Once they are gone, I can continue. They are waiting for me to turn around.

One of the soldiers knows a few words in English. He explains that I am in dangerous country and that I should not be here. They will escort me back to the last well.

I tell him I will follow behind them.

He says no I will not. I will ride in front of them.

I consider shutting off my bike and sitting down on a rock in the incandescent heat. Taking out my lunch and eating slowly, looking around, waiting them out. But they don't look like the type to put up with this routine. The well isn't that far back. If nothing else I can camp nearby and slip out at night.

They follow right on my tail. Along the way there are places where I could dart into a narrow wadi and evade them and even if they started shooting, I would probably get away, but I think better of it.

At the well there are two vehicles, another military Land Cruiser and an unmarked Land Rover. My escort sidles up beside its counterpart and windows come down. I ignore them and stop near the well. I prop up my bike and begin to untie my backpack.

A lean white man steps out of the Land Rover and walks over to me. He is in wrinkled khakis and without a hat even though he is bald and the sun is malevolent. His eyes are a shocking white-blue. He introduces himself. I don't quite catch the name. A Scandinavian on contract with someone. He doesn't exactly say.

"You have come this far, so you can obviously do what you want."

"Thank you."

I ask him what's going on. He says the Tuaregs attacked a small village where there were a couple of development workers. They didn't kill anyone. They tied up the foreigners and ran off with one vehicle, one motorcycle, and one moped.

He is friendly. We slip into a larger discussion about what is really happening in the desert. He says it's complicated. The Tuaregs want their own country. They want the Sahara. Their homeland was drawn and quartered by colonists—

Algeria annexed the north, Mali the south, Mauritania the west, Niger and Libya the east—and they want it back.

He says he has suspicions that Libya is providing arms to rebel factions. I say that the Tuaregs seem to be the only people who could possibly live in the desert, so why not just let them have it.

"Well, yes, but . . ." He pauses and gives me an odd smile. "You see, there are these nasty rumors that oil has been discovered somewhere out here, somewhere deep in the dunes."

He points with his chin in the direction I have just been escorted in from.

"I see."

"Of course oil is like gold, isn't it." He grins, but his eyes are as cold as snow. "Makes people do crazy things."

I don't trust him but I like him. He has bigger issues to deal with than me. I'm just another wayward traveler. I decide I can be honest. I tell him I want to go to Timbuktu and ask him what he thinks.

"I think they will track you down."

He says my motorcycle is too valuable. They will follow me and find me. They may or may not kill me, probably not. It is unnecessary.

"They will simply take your motorcycle. The desert will do the rest."

The Land Rover honks.

"Excuse me." I stare into his eyes. "Who are *they*?"

He lowers his head, then looks up. "Good luck."

He stands and salutes casually, flicking out two fingers in front of his forehead. I realize he is not as old as I thought. He has just been out in the desert so long it has lacerated his face.

He walks back to the Land Rover. Somebody inside opens the door for him and hands him his sunglasses. He shuts his door and the Land Rover pulls in front of the two Land Cruisers. Something is exchanged, then all three drive off into the desert.

I spend the night at the well thinking.

Sometimes you want people to care about you but sometimes you don't. If they care about you, it clouds their judgment. This man, whoever he was, didn't care in the least about me. He was not trying to scare me. Whatever happened to me was my own problem.

In the morning I get out the map. I am still on the north side of the Niger. On the south side of the river there appear to be several stretches of road that hopscotch toward Timbuktu.

Why not? I turn around and head south.

When I drop into the Niger floodplain, I am stymied over and over by great strips of muddy water. Each time I eventually find a fisherman with a dugout and hire him to pole me and my motorbike across. It is two days before I ride up onto the southern shore of the Niger, find a piece of highway and hook north.

Somewhere beyond a village called Douentza I come upon a roadblock. This time there are several jeeps and a troop truck and dozens of soldiers. They point their guns at me and tell me to turn around, and I do.

I know I could go around them. There are no fences, no trenches, no barbwire. The desert is open. I could simply backtrack a few miles, turn left, ride out into the desert for twenty miles, turn left again, and continue northward. I am tempted. But I am also not stupid. No sense getting killed. Not when there's another way. The Niger flows right by Timbuktu.

Back to the river.

THE MYTH

I have been on this ship for three days and three nights. The ship is overflowing with passengers. From the sheer weight of humanity the vessel rides deep in the river.

It is midafternoon and I am staring down from my perch into the water. We have been docked for hours and the water has become fouled. Women hold their children over the side to vomit. Men and boys piss over the side. Girls dump the tin cans their families shit in overboard. Everything goes into the river. Rinds and bottles and packaging and puddles of motor oil float on the surface like debris from a shipwreck.

There are five decks to this ark and every one is packed. Each family has strung up partitions of bright fabric to create their own compartment. Inside they unroll reed mats and fit them together like tile. This is their home for the course of the journey. They take off their shoes before entering. The men lie back using their turbans as pillows. The women squat over tin ovens fanning the embers and suckling their children. The kids race through the tunnels that connect the catacombs.

When I boarded at Mopti, I climbed directly to the top deck. I have taken ferries in Africa before and know the hierarchy; it is similar to that of the theater. The closer you are to the performance, or the better your perspective, the more expensive the seat. On a ferry the performance is the immense sweep of land, water, and sky and the best vantage

point is the top deck. The penniless and the sick in body or
soul occupy the lower levels. The wealthy purchase cabin
berths on the top deck. In between are all the rest of us
squabbling for a few square feet of our own.

I knew the top deck would be mobbed but from the pier
I could see crates stacked out on the prow. The crane oper-
ator had loaded them haphazardly. When I got up to the top
deck, it was a ghetto, so solidly populated and complexly
subdivided it would have been trespassing to cross over to
the crates. So I climbed over the railing. Hanging four
stories above the water, feet on one rail and hands gripping
the other, my pack dangling from my back, I inched my way
out to the prow.

Sure enough, I found a space among the crates. An
enclosed balcony. An aerie right on the edge, just big
enough for me to lie down in. I unrolled my foam pad and
rigged up a canopy with the fly of my tent and have been
living here ever since. It's the best seat in the house.

For over an hour, barefoot stevedores have been humping sacks of cement onto the ship. They trudge up a long
wooden plank that runs from the foot-plowed mud of the
bank up into the bowels of the vessel. One bag upon one
bent back, their sweat spilling off their noses into the water.

But they are not the only ones on the plank. Dozens of
vendors flow in and out carrying an entire market on their
heads, cucumbers to cow balls. Once a girl stepped in the
way of a stevedore and he elbowed her off the plank into
the river. Now hundreds of lemons bob in the water along
with all the garbage.

The sun is beginning to set. Already. Time is like water. I
peel an orange and eat it. I brought my own food for the
trip, but because the ticket included meals, I did eat in the
dining room once.

A platter was placed on every table. On each platter was
a hand-packed mound of orange rice. Everyone ate with
their right hand without speaking, squeezing the rice into
balls and pushing them into their mouths. After we left, the
workers scraped the leftovers back onto the platters using

the sides of their hands like spatulas. Then they repacked the rice into new orange cones. Then the platters were lowered by dumbwaiter to the deck below, and served.

Every day the orange cones have descended from deck to deck until all the rice is eaten. On the upper deck the meals are sparsely attended and the platters are loaded. On the lower levels the dining rooms are desperately crowded and the platters are immediately empty.

And now it is dusk. The stevedores are gone but the plank has not been raised, people with baskets hawking this or that are still moving back and forth in the darkling. I lie down along the edge and turn my head and look out across the desert.

Tomorrow we will reach the village of Kabara, the port of Timbuktu. It will not be the way I imagined it. I imagined myself appearing all alone out of the emptiness of the desert, entering Timbuktu soundlessly on my red motor-cycle. I thought it would be fitting. But I was wrong. I sold my motorcycle in the city of Djenné to a woman named Joanne Wedum. She works for CARE, helping women grow alternative crops. For three years she has been crisscrossing her district imprisoned in a jeep with a male chauffeur. The motorcycle set her free to do her business.

Tomorrow I will enter Timbuktu, but tonight I will dream of Sue. Up in my nest above the water breathing the black desert air letting the ferry bear me through the night as quietly as a falling star sinks through the sky. I have dreamed of Sue every night since boarding this ship, as if it were carrying me back home. As if this river were flowing across continents.

Tiny fires are springing up all over the deck now. It is dinnertime. The ship has not moved. We have been docked here all day.

I roll onto my shoulder and look over the prow down along the side of the ship. Hundreds of people line the decks. They are dropping tin cans overboard on rope or lengths of wire. They let the cans fill, haul them up hand over hand, then raise the liquid to their lips.

Everyone draws their water from the river. The river is all there is.

I disembark at Kabara and walk to Timbuktu. It is seven miles north of the Niger and takes me two hours. As I approach, coming along an asphalt two-lane lined with trees, I see Timbuktu looks like any other medium-size mud village, brown.

In the dunes on the outskirts of town I find a building that rents rooms to travelers. It is like a castle. There are three floors all with loggias open to an inner courtyard. The courtyard is dirt, three skinny trees, two plastic chairs. The rooms are as cold and spare as the cells in a monastery—an arched doorway, a naked bed with a straw mattress, a rectangular hole in the outer wall that would look out onto the desert if the shutters were not locked. There are dozens of rooms in this fortress but I see no one. I pay a gnarled woman and she gives me a key wired to a tab of wood.

I go to the top floor, find the stairs that spiral up through the ceiling onto the mud roof, walk out to the corner that overlooks Timbuktu, and set up my tent.

On the ground floor there is a dark mossy room with a pipe stuck out from the wall at waist level. I take a cold shower, brush my teeth, put my sweaty clothes back on, and wander into town.

Mohammed finds me immediately. I am strolling through the hot sand looking around and happen to stop on a corner and he hobbles right up to me as if this were the place we'd agreed to meet.

"I am guide." He pronounces it geed. "I am good guide."

Mohammed is standing on one leg leaning on a primitive crutch. His other leg is curled around the crutch like a shriveled vine.

"I don't need a guide."

"Every man need guide."

"Not me."

"No"—he makes a funny face—"you need guide."

I turn the corner and keep walking and he follows me.

"You not know where you going?"

"I am where I am going."

Mohammed laughs gaily and kicks his good foot in the sand.

"Ha, not possible."

He spots two German tourists at the next corner and limps quickly over to them and offers his services. He speaks in German. They curse him. He catches back up with me.

"How old are you, Mohammed?"

"I am sixteen years."

"How many languages do you speak?"

"Five, maybe six."

"How did you learn them?"

He grins. "I am Timbuktu guide!"

He asks me if I am hungry. I say I am.

"What do you like to eat?"

"I eat what you eat."

It is a test and he knows it.

He guides me down a dark alley to a hole in the wall where a caldron is set in a block of tile. A man is sitting crosslegged on a pillow sliding sticks into a hole at the base of the block of tile. Two men in turbans, blue cloth wound around their heads with only slits for their eyes and lips, are drinking from wooden bowls. When they are done, they set the bowls down and the man dips a ladle into the steaming caldron, refills them, and hands them to us. From a thick disk of bread he tears off two large chunks and holds them out to us. I take one and Mohammed takes the other and we both dip them into our soup and eat.

Mohammed becomes my guide. For the next week he leads me through Timbuktu. All the streets are narrow and crooked and deep in sand but he hobbles easily ahead of me. Every day we eat every meal together. Every night I pay him and he disappears into the darkness.

209

He shows me to a house that is being built from manure and mud and explains in detail how it is done. He shows me homes with carved doors armored with brass spikes and then takes me to the woodshop where the doors are made. He directs me to a school where the boys richer than he are studying. We stand outside the window and listen to them.

He guides me to a small cooperative where nine women are working with sewing machines, pooling their money for a day care center.

We take a bus outside town to see a new irrigation project that is growing vegetables with water sucked up out of the Niger with diesel pumps. On the way back we get off the bus early and he introduces me to a man who is an expert bricklayer. The man says he has spent his life inside wells fitting bricks into a circular puzzle so tight not a drop of water is ever lost.

These are the things I asked to see. But Mohammed is not only a linguist and a pragmatist; he is an historian. We use one day going mosque to mosque. Sidi Yehia, named after the famous marabout buried beneath its foundation in 1462. Sankore, surrounded by young boys chanting verses from the Koran. Dyingereyber, built in 1336 by an architect who returned from Cairo with Mansa Musa.

One evening he leads me to a nondescript building that turns out to be a library housing some of the ancient texts of Timbuktu. For hundreds of years Timbuktu was the center of learning for all of West Africa. Mohammed reads to me from the tomes. Stories of the desert. Stories of history. He shows me the pages purled with recursive Arabesque patterns.

On the last day Mohammed takes me around to see the houses where the famous white explorers stayed. The first one is that of Heinrich Barth, a German who spent five years traveling in the Sahara in the 1850s. There is a metal plaque above the door.

Only a few lanes away is the house where Major Gordon Laing stayed. Another faded metal plaque above the door.

I ask him why there are these special plaques commemorating forgotten white men. I want to know what he thinks.

"Because they were the first *white* men to come to my town." Then he grins. "But we were here all along."

The last house Mohammed shows me is where René Caillie stayed.

Caillie began his journey in Guinea. He boated up the Rio Nunez, hired a Malinke guide named Ibrahim and joined a small caravan traveling inland. To cross the Fouta Djallon, Caillie replaced Ibrahim with a new guide, Lamfia. After three months Caillie reached the Niger River at Kouroussa. He had malaria and was shivering uncontrollably.

Although there were pirogues on the Niger at Kouroussa, the main trade route continued overland. Caillie went on to Kankan where he hired a new guide named Arafamba. Together they joined another eastbound caravan. By this time Caillie, having worn through his sandals, was walking barefoot.

A month later he limped into a village called Tieme. He had acute malaria, could not eat, and his left foot was deeply ulcerated. In exchange for a pair of scissors he was given a small hut infested with maggots. Had it not been for the kindness of a woman Caillie called Manman, he would have died. This dried, toothless grandmother took pity on the diseased stranger. Every day for a month she applied a poultice of baobab leaves to his wounds and dripped herbal stew into him.

Caillie arrived in Tieme early in August 1827. By November he had survived the malaria through heavy doses of "kinine" and his foot was beginning to heal. Then came scurvy.

The roof of my mouth became quite bare, a part of the bone exfoliated and fell away, and my teeth seemed ready to fall out of their sockets. I felt that my brain would be affected by the excruciating pains I felt in my head, and I was more than a fortnight without sleep. To crown my misery the sore on my foot broke out again . . . I was reduced to a skeleton. . . . One thought alone absorbed my mind—that of Death. I wished for it and prayed for it to God.

Again Manman nursed him back to life.

Caillie left Tieme with a trading caravan in January 1828. In March he entered Djenné, the fortressed island city in the middle of the Niger. From Djenné it was not possible to travel by land to Timbuktu. The Tuaregs owned the desert. Caillie boarded a colossal pirogue—ninety feet long, twelve feet wide, drawing six feet. The vessel was heavily laden with rice, millet, cotton, and slaves. He was given a shelf belowdecks among the slaves, a space so small he could not lie down.

It is five hundred miles downriver from Djenné to Kabara. Tuareg pirates regularly forced themselves onto the boat and demanded tribute. Fearing they might kill him if he were discovered, the slaves hid Caillie beneath mats and blankets.

One month after leaving Djenné, on 25 April 1828, René Caillie reached Kabara and walked into Timbuktu. He had been traveling alone, light, often barefoot, for exactly one year.

I looked around and found that the sight before me did not answer my expectations. I had formed a totally different idea of the grandeur and wealth of Timbuktu. . . . The city presented, at first view, nothing but a mass of ill-looking houses built of earth. Nothing was seen in all directions but immense plains of quicksand of yellowish-white colour. The sky was pale red as far as the horizon.

He stayed in Timbuktu for ten days, taking notes on the city's size, customs, mosques, and commerce. He was told the story of an infidel named Laing who had entered Timbuktu two years before, refused to accept Mohammed as the prophet of God, and was beheaded.

He left Timbuktu with a large caravan in May 1828, believing the worst of his sufferings were over. He was wrong. He was crossing the Sahara in the summer. Temperatures could reach 160 degrees Fahrenheit. The route north to Morocco was a thousand miles long with fewer than twenty wells. Within days Caillie was suffering from extreme thirst. He thought of nothing but water. "Rivers, streams, rivulets were the only ideas that presented themselves to my mind." He was limited to a ration of less than a pint of foul black liquid a day. It took three months to reach Morocco. Caillie arrived alive, but only barely. He was so emaciated his bones protruded through his skin.

When René Caillie returned to France, he was a national hero. He was awarded the 10,000-franc prize from the Geographical Society of Paris, given a 6,000-franc pension by the French government, made a Chevalier of the Legion of Honour by King Charles X.

He then went back to the home of his youth, Mauze, and wrote his own adventure book, *Travels Through Central Africa to Timbuctoo*.

Six years later, at the age of thirty-nine, plagued by disorders contracted during his journeys in Africa, he died.

Alas, René Caillie could not write like Daniel Defoe or Mungo Park. He was an extraordinary man who wrote in an ordinary way. He had not set out for Timbuktu with the blessing and financing of a government or learned society. He had not attempted to ennoble his journey by disguising it as a scientific endeavor. Worst of all, his descriptions of Timbuktu did not fit the image cradled like a holy grail in the mind of the public. How could the most mysterious city in history be nothing more than a collection of mud buildings, a mere trading post in the desert? Impossible.

René Caillie was deemed a fake, a charlatan, and soon forgotten.

Myth, always and forever, is greater than fact.

It is time to go home. I can feel the tugging. I am being drawn back in like a kite.

Mohammed said he wished me to have dinner with his family before I left. He said he would come for me in the evening.

I am waiting on the roof of the castle. I thought I would write in my journal but I have nothing more to say. I close the book and look out over Timbuktu. After a while I turn and look north, into the dunes, into the desert. Once you find the patience, there is always a drama being performed out there.

Twilight is beginning, descending upon the landscape. The earth is changing color. The sweetness of peach to the lust of auburn, the gentleness of mauve to the stillness of lavender, the certainty of azure, the denouement of black. Then the resurrection: pinholes in the welkin as if there were light on the other side if we could ever get there.

He said he would come; he will come. I sit on the mud roof in the night and wait.

Then I hear him.

Thok ssss thok ssss thok ssss.

He is hopping himself up the stairs. As I stand up, he passes out of the cupola into the starlight, hobbling toward me across the roof.

"*Salaam alaikum, Marcos.*"

"*Alaikum el Salaam, Mohammed.*"

He wheels around, his caftan whispering, and I follow him back down the stairwell into the street.

We walk silently through black corridors, the river of night above our heads. Mohammed moves swift and sure-footed, as if his crutch were flesh. There are no streetlamps in Africa so we all must learn to walk in the dark. It is an act of faith. To simply move your legs and let your feet find the path.

He is guiding me to the outskirts of Timbuktu. The lanes become deep with sand. The desert is trying to take back the city, gradually filling it up like an hourglass.

At the end of a lane that disappears into the desert there is a campfire. On either side are ruins—mud buildings with their roofs gone and their insides drifted in. There are a dozen people around the fire. They are Mohammed's family. We pass into the circle and Mohammed introduces me to each person. I shake their hands one by one. The old men are placid; the women accept me with their eyes; the children giggle.

A space is made for me in the circle and a rug laid upon the sand. I am asked to sit. Over the fire is a dark kettle. Beside it on the ground is an aluminum platter heaped with millet. The platter is passed to me and I pinch out a clump with my right hand, form it into balls and put them into my mouth. Everyone watches me. They ask me to eat more and I do. Then the platter is replaced near the fire. Using large wooden spoons two women lift the head of a goat from the kettle and drop it onto the platter.

Mohammed explains that the brains and the eyes are the delicacy and that I am the guest of honor. I remove one of the eyeballs with my fingers and eat it. Mohammed plucks out the other, swallowing it whole. We eat the brains together.

After the psalm of tea the questions begin. Mohammed translates. The old men want to know what life is like in my faraway home. Timbuktu is their home. They want to know about distant and mysterious places.

The women want to know if I am married, if I have children. I show them a picture of Sue. They crowd together and hold it at an angle to catch the firelight. When I tell them she is pregnant, they coo and gaze at me and smile. They are glad for me for they know the adventure of children.

Their children, Mohammed's younger brothers and

sisters and cousins, are all sitting crosslegged, watching me, waiting patiently. I know what they are waiting for.

My journey is over. It was physical and finite. Now it shall pass through the lake of the mind and be transformed into something incorporeal and eternal: a story.

I start slowly. Finding the source, assembling our boats, fighting through the bush. It draws them in. Their dark little heads slide forward and their eyes begin to widen. My words are coming out of Mohammed's mouth but their faces are fixed upon me. The tale of the croc makes them suck in their cheeks.

I have them all, even the adults, except for one child. An infant, a tiny boy not a year old. The boy is naked. His skin the color of the earth, his hair curly and black. He is a healthy baby with a round belly and bunches of fat between his legs. He has just learned to walk and the world has become his. He keeps squirming out of his mother's grasp. Whenever he escapes, he leans forward until he begins to fall, then his little bowlegged legs start moving and his tiny feet shuffle in short quick steps. But he doesn't get far before someone jumps up and grabs him and brings him back.

The story continues. The faces of the children glow in the firelight. They grab each other when the hippo charges into the water. When I get to the part about the bees, some of them hold their hands over their faces and the old men laugh and the women sigh. When I go over the waterfall, the men are staring at me hard and the women are shaking their heads and the children have their mouths open.

Then someone shouts. The baby is gone. We all spring to our feet and spin away from the fire and look out into the desert.

There he is, screaming with laughter, waddling as fast as he can straight into the dark, straight into the unknown.

CODA

Kourou and Fali had twins, a girl and a boy, Hawa and Adam. A year later Kourou bought a motorcycle. His business is still good.

John Haines and Rick Smith paddled out of the Niger delta into the Gulf of Guinea and became the first men to run the Niger River, source to sea. Back home, John went to work for a nonprofit organization giving small loans to inner-city mothers. Rick returned to his carpentry.

Mike and I were present at the births of our firstborns. Mike and Diana had a son, Justin. Sue and I had a daughter, Addi. They plunged into the world two weeks apart and are steadfast friends. They like to go camping together. Addi brings her stuffed kitty and Justin brings his dinosaurs.

Mike and I did go to Tibet on our next trip. Diana and Sue were pregnant again. It would be our last journey together.

One night in Lhasa I awoke suddenly, entirely alert. I could hear Mike breathing and snapped on my headlamp.

"You want to hear the ocean, Buck?"

"Mike, *no!*"

He had lived through pulmonary edema before and he would live through it now, but by the time he flew out of Tibet, Mike could manage only a few steps before stopping to breathe. His lungs were almost full. I was scared to death. He kept cracking jokes, whispering them because that's all he could do, getting me to smile before lapsing into hacking and bubbling.

Several months after Tibet, Mike and Diana had twins, a girl and a boy, Carlie and Kevin. Sue and I had a second daughter, Teal.

In 1995, Mike and I went to Canada on separate expeditions. Me to climb, he to boat. Mike had finally conceded that climbing high mountains was too dangerous for him.

Mike and his younger brother Dan, Sharon Kava, and Brad Humphrey flew to Baffin Island in August. Their expedition had two parts. First they would cross the Barnes Icecap, then sail Hobie Cats down the east coast of Baffin Island. They had spent the summer training on the alpine lakes in Wyoming: running their boats into icebergs, tipping them over, righting them, tipping over again, swimming for miles in their dry suits.

The first part of the expedition went without a hitch. They crossed the Barnes Icecap never using the shotguns they brought for protection against polar bears. When they reached the head of Gibbs Fjord, where they intended to begin boating, the Hobie Cats had not been delivered. They radioed Jushua Illuaq, an Inuit Eskimo guide they had hired. He said the boats, along with all the dry suits, were lost in the mail. They waited for a week but the boats didn't arrive. When they were out of food, Jushua picked them up in a small motorboat.

En route home, in the Arctic Ocean off the Remote Peninsula of eastern Baffin Island, they encountered a pod of bowhead whales. For reasons no one will ever know, a whale breached beneath them, capsizing their boat. They had life jackets but no dry suits. Jushua was wearing an insulated survival suit and would be found three days later, alive.

The temperature of the ocean was just above freezing and the motorboat could not be righted. They held on to each other, arms linked over the hull, talking to each other, giving each other encouragement. They held on for as long as they could. Then one by one, Sharon and Brad and Dan and Mike perished. Mike was the last to die, on 2 September 1995. He was thirty-seven.

We were as brothers, Mike and I. Best friends. Mark and Mike. We chose each other and were perfectly matched. We grew up together, became men together, became fathers together. As I wrote this book, I would read it to Mike, checking my memory. Often we laughed so hard we cried.

Mike and I had big plans. Trips with our families to Africa, New Zealand, Alaska. Although we seldom spoke of it, we intended to grow old together. Make the long journey together.

There are so many stories I have not told. These are for our children now. Around a campfire beneath the stars. Someday I will tell them this one.

It was fall in Wyoming. Cobalt days and cutting nights, the time of precarious balance just before the skies tip and winter pours in. It was too cold for kayaking or rock climbing and there wasn't enough snow for ski touring. We went out anyway, just the two of us, up into the mountains. It was one of our first adventures together. We didn't have a plan. We didn't know where we were going or where we'd end up.

We brought along our new ice axes and our new rope. They were used but they were new to us. We'd bought them at a yard sale in a trailer court out in the prairie. The ice axes had wooden shafts and the rope was short and had been used for breaking wild horses. The owner was a cowboy. He said when he got married his wife had made him stop climbing. He smirked. We couldn't understand how he could let somebody do that to him.

We struck out at daybreak dressed head to toe in wool. Inside our rucksacks were goosedown coats our moms had sewn from kits, canteens of Kool-Aid and sandwiches in waxed paper. I carried the rope in a coil over one shoulder. We could have tied the ice axes onto our packs but we were too proud of them. We carried them in our hands like battle axes and felt prepared for anything, anything at all.

We found an unknown river and started following it through the mountains just to see where it went. It gradually cut a canyon in the rock. We followed it all day, the walls rising above us. By dusk we stood below a sheer face that blocked our passage. The river ran into the wall, spread out and curled around. We could keep going only if we crossed over to the far bank.

We didn't know how deep the river was. We couldn't tell. It was skinned with ice. The ice was less than an inch thick, impossible to walk on. We'd already crashed through leaping along the bank, freezing our leather boots and woolen pant legs solid as cordwood.

We weren't sure how to get across to the other side, but we had a hunch. We did rock-paper-scissors and Mike won. He tied the rope around his waist and slid his ice ax down between the pack and his back.

I held the rope. Several feet back from the ice, on the round river rocks, Mike lay down on his stomach. Spreading his arms and legs apart, he began sliding forward, pulling with his fingers and pushing with his toes. In this position he inched his way out onto the ice . . . and it didn't break! It bent, bowed under his weight like a sheet of white plastic. We couldn't believe it. It was as if he had defied the laws of physics.

Once Mike's feet pushed off from the stones on the bank, he had no way of moving. The ice was too slick. For a moment he lay still, thinking, spread out on the ice as if he were dropping through clouds. Then, very slowly, he reached behind his head and drew out his ax. Grasping the shaft at the base, he held the ax out in front of him, gently nicked the ice with the pick, hooked the hole and pulled himself forward.

He repeated this move again and again, dragging himself out across the ice. Once he said, "I can see right through. I can see the water moving underneath me. It's beautiful, deep too."

It was almost dark. The sky had turned purple and a few stars had come out. The black cold of winter was dropping into the canyon. Before he was halfway across, I had to yell at him. He was out of rope.

"Drop the rope," he shouted. He didn't look back.

"What if you fall through?"

"Drop the rope!"

I tied myself into the rope and I slid my ax down behind my neck. I laid myself on the ground, spread my arms and legs out, and began sliding forward onto the ice.

When Mike felt slack in the rope he started moving ahead again, unhesitating, going for the other side. Then he must have known something was up because he stopped, raised his head, and peered backward over his shoulder. His wild red hair was frozen in his face and his eyes were the color of the water streaming below us. He grinned at me.

"Buck, some folks might think we're on thin ice."

We started laughing and whooping and the sound echoed up through the dark canyon.

Then Mike passed over to the other side.

SOURCES

Altenhofer, Christian, and Ursula Altenhofer. *Der Hadern-kahn: Geschichte des Faltbootes*. Oberschleissheim: Pollner Verlag, 1989.

Beston, Henry. *The Book of Gallant Vagabonds*. London: Werner Laurie, 1925.

Bovill, E. W. *The Niger Explored*. New York: Oxford University Press, 1968.

——. *The Golden Trade of the Moors*, 2nd ed. New York: Oxford University Press, 1968.

Brent, Peter. *Black Nile*. London: Gordon and Cremonesi, 1977.

Caillie, René. *Travels Through Central Africa to Timbuctoo*. London: Cass, 1968.

Gardner, Brian. *The Quest for Timbuctoo*. New York: Harcourt, Brace and World, 1968.

Gramont, Sanche de. *The Strong Brown God: The Story of the Niger River*. Boston: Houghton Mifflin, 1976.

Hibbert, Christopher. *Africa Explored: 1769–1889*. New York: Penguin Books, 1984.

Ledyard, John. *A Journal of Captain Cook's Last Voyage*. Hartford: Nathaniel Patten, 1779.

——. *Journey Through Russia and Siberia, 1787–88*. Madison: University of Wisconsin Press, 1966.

Lupton, Kenneth. *Mungo Park the African Traveler*. Oxford, U.K.: Oxford University Press, 1979.

McLynn, Frank. *Hearts of Darkness: The European*

Exploration of Africa. New York: Carrol and Graf, 1992.

Mason, Bill. *Path of the Paddle.* Toronto: Key Porter Books, 1980.

Miner, Horace. *The Primitive City of Timbuctoo.* Princeton, N.J.: American Philosophical Society, 1953.

Park, Mungo. *Travels into the Interior of Africa.* London: Dent, 1954.

Ross, Michael. *Cross the Great Desert.* London: Gordon and Cremonesi, 1977.

Rotberg, Robert I. *Africa and Its Explorers: Motives, Methods, and Impact.* Cambridge, Mass.: Harvard University Press, 1970.

Severin, Timothy. *The African Adventure.* New York: Dutton, 1973.

Zimmerly, David W. *Qajaq: Kayaks of Siberia and Alaska.* Juneau, Alaska: Division of State Museums, 1986.